Helion & Company Limited
Unit 8 Amherst Business Centre
Budbrooke Road
Warwick
CV34 5WE
England
Tel. 01926 499 619
Email: info@helion.co.uk
Website: www.helion.co.uk
Twitter: @helionbooks
Visit our blog http://blog.helion.co.uk/

Text © José Augusto Matos and Zélia Oliveira 2024
Photographs © as individually credited
Colour artwork © David Bocquelet, Luca Canossa, Tom Cooper, Anderson Subtil 2024
Map © Tom Cooper 2024

Designed and typeset by Farr out Publications, Wokingham, Berkshire
Cover design Paul Hewitt, Battlefield Design (www.battlefield-design.co.uk)

Every reasonable effort has been made to trace copyright holders and to obtain their permission for the use of copyright material. The author and publisher apologise for any errors or omissions in this work, and would be grateful if notified of any corrections that should be incorporated in future reprints or editions of this book.

ISBN 978-1-804514-92-4

British Library Cataloguing-in-Publication Data
A catalogue record for this book is available from the British Library

All rights reserved. No part of this publication may be reproduced, stored in a retrieval system, or transmitted, in any form, or by any means, electronic, mechanical, photocopying, recording or otherwise, without the express written consent of Helion & Company Limited.

We always welcome receiving book proposals from prospective authors.

CONTENTS

Abbreviations		2
Introduction		2
1	Win Or Be Defeated	3
2	The First Rebellion	11
3	Between Tanks And Flowers	27
Sources and Bibliography		56
Notes		58
About the Authors		66

Note: In order to simplify the use of this book, all names, locations and geographic designations are as provided in *The Times World Atlas*, or other traditionally accepted major sources of reference, as of the time of described events.

ABBREVIATIONS

CEMGFA	*Chefe do Estado-Maior General das Forças Armadas* (Chief of Staff of the Armed Forces)	**JSN**	*Junta de Salvação Nacional* (National Salvation Junta)
CIA	Central Intelligence Agency	**MFA**	*Movimento das Forças Armadas* (Armed Forces Movement)
CICA 1	Auto 1 Instruction and Driving Centre		
CIOE	*Centro de Instrução de Operações Especiais* (Special Operations Troops Centre)	**PC**	*Posto de Comando* (Command Post)
		PCP	*Partido Comunista Português* (Portuguese Communist Party)
CNT	*Centro Nacional de Transmissões* (National Transmission Centre)	**PIDE/DGS**	*Polícia Internacional e de Defesa do Estado/ Direcção Geral de Segurança* (International and State Defence Police/Directorate General for Security)
EPA	*Escola Prática de Artilharia* (Artillery Practical School)		
EPAM	*Escola Prática de Administração Militar* (Military Administration Practical School)	**PSP**	*Polícia de Segurança Pública* (Public Security Police)
EPC	*Escola Prática de Cavalaria* (Cavalry Practical School)	**RC**	*Regimento de Cavalaria* (Regiment of Cavalry)
EPI	*Escola Prática de Infantaria* (Infantry Practical School)	**RCP**	*Rádio Clube Português* (Portuguese Radio Club)
EPT	*Escola Prática de Transmissões* (Transmission Practice School)	**RTP**	*Rádio Televisão Portuguesa* (Radio Television Portugal)
FAP	*Força Aérea Portuguesa* (Portuguese Air Force)	**STM**	*Serviço de Transmissões Militares* (Military Telecommunications Service)
GNR	*Guarda Nacional Republicana* (National Republican Guard)		

INTRODUCTION

In March 1974, a climate of conspiracy reigned in Portugal. Marcello Caetano, who was in charge of the government, insisted on the continuation of the Portuguese presence in Africa. For him, it made no sense for Portugal to leave the African colonies, abandoning the European population living there to their own fate. But to maintain the Portuguese presence, Caetano had to continue the war against the liberation movements, which consumed more and more of the nation's resources. Costa Gomes and Spínola, the two generals at the top of the military hierarchy, did not share this view. Spínola, with Costa Gomes's permission, had published a book that questioned the policy that had been followed until then, causing a real political earthquake. Caetano saw the book as an affront and offered his resignation to the President of the Republic, Américo Thomaz, but the latter did not accept the leader of the government's resignation and reiterated his confidence in Caetano. To legitimise his policy, the head of the executive sought the support of the deputies in the National Assembly, who approved a motion of acceptance of the overseas policy. From then on, Caetano felt his actions were legitimised. On the domestic front, however, the captains' movement

One of the striking features of the Portuguese revolution was popular support. On 25 April thousands of people were in the streets of Lisbon cheering rebel soldiers and offering them flowers and food after the troops overthrew the government of Premier Marcello Caetano. Some of the crowd here can be seen standing atop an EBR 75 armoured car. (Miranda Castela collection/Archive of the Assembly of the Republic)

continued to plot against the regime. Tired of the war in Africa and of the government's inability to solve the overseas problem, the conspirators now only thought of overthrowing the dictatorship. To this end, they prepared plans for a military coup. The removal of Spínola and Costa Gomes by the regime accelerated the plans of the captains, who began to show clear signs of great dissatisfaction. The dismissal of the two generals for refusing to participate in a ceremony in support of government policy, provoked the first military revolt on 16 March 1974, which was overpowered by the regime forces, but the second attempt on 25 April developed quickly and in less than 24 hours, the insurgents controlled the situation and Marcello Caetano was surrounded in his refuge by rebel forces led by a young captain. Surrender was inevitable and the ruler ended up handing over power into the hands of General Spínola. The streets of Lisbon, already occupied by the troops of the movement, were also taken over by the people in an explosion of joy. A new era was beginning in Portugal.

In this second volume we report on the events from March 1974 until the fall of the regime and the establishment of the new military power. The book ends with the fall of the political police, the most hated institution of the old regime and the last to surrender. We use mainly archive material, as well as the memories of the protagonists who were on both sides of the barricade to draw a detailed picture of this period.

1
WIN OR BE DEFEATED

At the beginning of the second week of March 1974, the leader of the Portuguese government, Marcello Caetano, seemed more confident about continuing with his overseas policy in Africa after the approval obtained in the National Assembly a few days earlier. In a parliament dominated by regime-affiliated MPs, no other outcome was to be expected, but Marcello was now convinced he had the support of the nation's representatives to continue with the defence of the Overseas Territories. He probably also thought he had the support of the Armed Forces, but he sensed that this support hung by a thread and that the two generals at the top of National Defence had other ideas regarding the overseas problem. He had not fired them for fear of a revolt within the Army, but it was a problem he had to solve.

It was then that he sought out the President of the Republic Américo Thomaz, on 11 March, to officially inform him of the approved motion and of his concerns regarding the governmental activity. Marcello said that he wanted to continue with the governmental action and showed the President his concern with the economic situation, communicating that he intended to remodel the economic sector of the government, an intention he had for some time, but which he had postponed due to the incident with the publication of General Spínola's book.[1] Spínola was a well-known general and a man of the regime, but the book he published openly questioned Portuguese colonial policy in Africa and left the most conservative sectors of the regime in shock, as they could not understand why Caetano had not prevented its publication.

About this meeting, Thomaz wrote that on 11 March the political crisis raised by the publication of the book *Portugal e o Futuro* (*Portugal and the Future*) worsened during that day's audience with the head of the government, the first after the one on 28 February. Américo Thomaz began by regretting that he had not been aware of the publication and blamed Marcello Caetano for the book's publication.[2]

This was the second hearing to start on the subject of the book. On 28 February, Thomaz had referred to its inconvenient diffusion, but 11 days later he set out to hold the President of the Council directly responsible, after realising the repercussions, having listened to his most direct advisors and the situation in the Armed Forces remaining unchanged, with no sanction applied to the two generals, who had been complicit in the publication of the controversial book. Thomaz said that Caetano seemed to have panicked when he told

Spínola was a man of the regime, but the book he published in 1974 openly questioned Portugal's colonial policy in Africa and caused a political earthquake in the country. (Revista do Povo collection)

him that he had to dismiss the generals. According to the President, Caetano reacted with an interrogation: 'how can I exonerate the two generals, if it was I who authorised the publication of the book?' Marcello's panic may be justified because he feared that, once the generals were dismissed, this situation would lead to a reaction from the younger officers, who he believed were under the control of António Spínola and Costa Gomes.

But for Thomaz, the publication of the book was no longer the essential issue for which they should be exonerated, since the book incident, although constituting a clear error and even a strange abuse, had already and unfortunately become *res judicata*! However, the reason was different, but decisive: they could not and should not remain at the head of the Armed Forces, 'two general officers who showed that they did not believe in the Portuguese military victory in Africa and who advocated a political solution, when it was precisely the military solution that the Nation, its Government and its Army were committed to from the beginning, for they did not consider any alternative solution admissible.'[3]

This time it would be Marcello who did not report this part of the meeting in his memoirs but noting that the conversation ended in an atmosphere of a certain tension, as never happened during the five and a half years in which they collaborated in those functions.[4] Thomaz confessed that he saw Caetano shaken after that conversation, foreseeing that he might want to precipitate his departure. That afternoon, Thomaz received a letter of resignation from Caetano in the following terms:

> Our conversation this morning has rooted in me the conviction that I should not continue at the head of the Government. I therefore ask Your Excellency to promote my replacement. I am effectively responsible for having told the Minister of Defence to rely on the information provided by General Costa Gomes to authorise the publication of General Spínola's book. For the error committed, I must pay. On the other hand, the criticisms made by Your Excellency of the Government's actions in various sectors are entirely justified and only prove that the fatigue of five and a half years, aggravated by a heart ailment, have deprived me of the necessary energy at this difficult moment in national life to conduct public business.[5]

The letter impressed Thomaz, who called the Ministers of Defence and of the Interior for advice and, after having heard them, asked Caetano to come to Belém at the end of the day. Together again, Thomaz would tell him that at that moment 'it is already late for any of them to abandon their office – we must go all the way – (that is, in reality either win or be defeated.)'

Caetano would only say in his memoirs that the second meeting on that tense day served to ratify Thomaz's confidence in his policy. However, the Head of State would write about Caetano's interpretation that his words were far from being a reiteration of trust, but that Marcello accepted them and never again spoke of resigning.

But the truth is that in less than two weeks it was already the second request for resignation made to the President of the Republic. The political crisis had reached rock bottom. It was now even clearer that Marcello was just trying to keep the government and the regime afloat. As Manuel José Homem de Mello, deputy in the National Assembly and a close associate of Caetano, would later say, 'the regime was dying, on the verge of dying, clinging to power only artificially.'[6]

Ministers No Longer in Control of Departments

At the same time as the crisis in Belém worsened, the Minister of Defence, Silva Cunha, called a meeting in his department for 11:00 am with the ministers of the Army, Andrade e Silva, of the Navy, Pereira Crespo, the Secretary of State for Aeronautics, Tello Polleri, the Under-Secretary of State for the Army, Viana de Lemos, and the Chief of Staff of the Armed Forces, Costa Gomes.

At the opening of the meeting, whose records were signed by Viana de Lemos, the Minister of Defence stated that the purpose was to study whether security measures should continue to be adopted in the Armed Forces to face the present situation and the degree that those measures should assume. He put the problem to the consideration of the military ministers.

The Minister of the Army informed that on that morning, at 8:00 a.m., the state of alert had been changed to a state of simple prevention at 9:00 p.m., and that the alert situation would be resumed the following morning, as long as the situation or the forecast of reactions to decisions that would be taken justified it. The Minister of the Navy generally agreed with this view but said that he opted for maintaining a single state of security, which could be the simple state of prevention, to avoid the disruptions caused by frequent changes. The Secretary of State for Aeronautics stated that he also preferred a single security status, which was later seconded by the Minister of the Army. Next, the Chief of Staff started by complaining about the lack of information that the General Internal Security Command struggled with, since it had not receive anything from the three branches' Chiefs of Staff, nor from the Security Forces, and little from the General Security Directorate. He stated that the situation was very serious and resulted from the fact that force measures had been taken that he considered inopportune for the present moment. From this part of Costa Gomes' intervention, it seemed to be noted that the CEMGFA (*Chefe do Estado-Maior General das Forças Armadas*, Chief of Staff of the Armed Forces), who should be one of the best informed of the regime, as the person responsible for the General Command of Internal Security, struggled with the lack of information and noted that there was an intention to deliberately not inform him on the part of the military ministers and the DGS. During the meeting, Costa Gomes gave an account of the path of the 'movement of captains' that had started as a reaction against the publication of Decree-Law no. 353 in 1973, which had originated the presentation of several claims. After the new governmental team had taken office, he had noted a trend that led to the conclusion that spirits were calming down, but lately that trend had been destroyed.

First, the incidents in Beira (Mozambique), between the civilian population and the military, had provoked a broad feeling of military solidarity that had spread to other overseas provinces and to metropolitan Portugal, a movement that was embodied in a manifesto with 470 signatures. He also considered as a factor responsible for the worsening of the situation the fact that a meeting of commands had been held at the Ministry of the Army, which he did not 'have the honour' to attend, as well as the measures taken lately with the transfer of some officers. He considered the situation to be extremely serious, due to the lack of acceptance by many soldiers of the hierarchical paths, as the generals lacked prestige, and he concluded that certainly none of the members of

Marcello Caetano and Américo Thomaz would be together until the end, but in the final phase of the regime, the old admiral would not cease to criticise Marcello for the way he managed the crisis created by Spínola and Costa Gomes. (*Diário de Notícias*)

the government present controlled the evolution of any situation within their department. He also asked for permission to present these considerations to the President of the Council in the presence of the Minister of Defence. Silva Cunha replied that the CEMGFA had access to the President of the Council, and that he could request a hearing without his presence, and that he considered that his comments went far beyond the scope of the meeting and could even be related to the equation of government policy.

Silva Cunha recalled that the policy was defined and the members of the government or the people they trusted had only one path left, and that was to follow it without hesitation. Personally, and with regard to the agitation of the captains, he distinguished three hypotheses: accepting their demands, which would imply the immediate abandonment of governmental functions, as this would be incompatible with the commitment of honour given when he accepted it; pretending that one ignored or did not understand what was happening, letting things get worse and ignoring that there were those who did not want to fight and preferred more comfortable situations and, finally, trying by all means to dominate the situation. Having in conscience the certainty that the policy followed by the government was the one that best suited the nation, he obviously could not accept the first two solutions. Silva Cunha thus put a brake on the discussion, expressing the desire that the debate should not become generalised in this scope and should be limited only to the subject that had been the object of the summons. However, it was clear that the minister was unaware of the gravity of the situation and the movements of the young officers who were actively plotting against the regime. Much more perceptive, Costa Gomes had already realised that the situation was serious and could bring additional problems to the government.

The Army Minister, Andrade e Silva, strongly supported the Defence Minister's position which he considered the only admissible one. He also clarified that the position taken regarding the officers who were transferred could in no way be considered dubious, since they had breached duties inscribed in the Military Discipline Regulation (RDM), which made them liable to disciplinary proceedings.

The Minister of the Navy, Pereira Crespo, in addition to expressing his agreement, asked that his vanity be forgiven but that, after five years in his department, he could not accept the statement that he would not be able to control his sector. The Secretary of State for Aeronautics supported the position and the thesis of the ministers of Defence and of the Army, stating that, personally, he would never want to be at the head of a department where command was from the bottom up, but he also stated that he had no doubt that he could control his department. The CEMGFA, Costa Gomes, stated that, although outside the scope of the meeting, he had intended to present his considerations and that he did so because he considered the situation in the three theatres of operations to be serious, saying that General Bettencourt Rodrigues (commander-in-chief in Guinea) returned to Bissau full of apprehensions. Finally, it was decided that the CEMGFA would communicate to the three branches that, until further notice, the units would remain in a state of alert.[7]

Costa Gomes' reference to General Bettencourt Rodrigues is interesting. He had in fact been in the metropolis in the first week of March, having met with the Minister of Defence on 6 and 7 March. In these meetings, Bettencourt Rodrigues learned about the rearmament and re-equipment plan of the Armed Forces, which according to the commander-in-chief of Guinea were in a dramatic situation. Rodrigues acknowledged that the PAIGC (*Partido*

PAIGC soldier with a rocket propelled grenade. The guerrillas fighting for the independence of Guinea-Bissau were well armed and a very serious threat to Portuguese troops. (Roel Coutinho collection)

Africano da Independência da Guiné e Cabo Verde, African Party for the Independence of Guinea and Cape Verde) had not been very active, but even so it had caused a high number of casualties among Portuguese troops. Moreover, they were always waiting for the guerrillas to carry out an action in force that further reduced the margin of initiative of the Portuguese forces. Some of the air assets, for maintenance reasons, were grounded, this being yet another factor reducing the Portuguese initiative. Rodrigues also complained about the lack of funds for the development plan in Guinea in which 10,500 contos were spent on personnel expenses leaving only 1,500 contos for other expenses.[8]

In his conversations with Silva Cunha, the Guinean military commander had been informed that the government was preparing to buy a range of war material that would be very useful in Guinea. On 4 March, Silva Cunha had sent a letter to his South African counterpart with information on the first purchases he intended to make under the South African loan, since under the terms of the loan agreement, Portugal always had to inform South Africa of the purchases it intended to make.[9] Accordingly, the letter contained a list of the type of armaments it was planning to buy for the Army and the Air Force. For the Army, the most relevant were mine detectors, 120mm, 81mm and 60mm mortars, 106mm recoilless cannons, as well as two platoons of the Crotale short-range air defence missile system. As for the Air Force, it was to receive new fighter jets (Mirage), light transport planes, more Alouette III and Puma helicopters, as well as various types of bombs and ammunition. At the end of the letter, Silva Cunha referred that the value to be spent on these acquisitions would be around 106 million rands (4.24 million contos).[10] This letter showed that the government was committed to providing the military forces with new combat means to face the guerrillas in Africa. Costa Gomes was aware of these steps and knew what was planned in terms of acquisitions, as he was directly involved in some of the negotiations.

However, Marcello was concerned with 'tidying up' the military issue and the problem he had with Costa Gomes and Spínola. He had before him the President of the Republic, pressured by the most conservative sectors to demand the dismissal of the two generals. On the other hand, he feared that once they were dismissed, the MFA (*Movimento das Forças Armadas*, Armed Forces Movement) would react in their defence. Caetano's reluctance to dismiss the two generals was reflected in two articles in the British press, written by

Portuguese soldiers in Guinea with mortar shells. The troops usually had 60mm light mortars and 81mm medium mortars at their disposal. However, Portuguese forces needed mortars with longer ranges and by 1974 the Ministry of Defence was arranging for their acquisition from Israel. (Archivio Famiglia Cristiana)

Bruce Loudon and published almost simultaneously: the first in the 10 March edition of *The Sunday Telegraph* and the second, on 11 March, in its sister paper, *The Daily Telegraph*. In the first article, the British journalist in Lisbon reported that the government had placed the military forces in a state of alert and that the current tension in the country was due to the consequences of the publication of Spínola's book two weeks before. According to the journalist, the publication of the book had been an affront to the right-wing of the regime identified with the President of the Republic and that there was pressure to dismiss the two generals, but that Caetano was reluctant to do so because some of Spínola's ideas were in line with the moderate policies of the head of the executive. In the words of the journalist, the President of the Council would have some sympathy for Spínola's federalist theses.[11]

The very next day, *The Daily Telegraph*, carried a very similar article by the same journalist, who once again stated that Spínola's book had provoked a serious internal crisis within the regime, the like of which had not been seen since the beginning of the war in Africa in 1961. Reading both articles, it is easy to see that there was a battle of factions within the regime between those who defended Spínola and those who criticised the general, who were grouped around Américo Thomaz. The journalist also mentioned that Caetano initially thought of resigning, but then tried to find a compromise solution between the two factions. To this end, he vigorously defended in the National Assembly the policy of gradual autonomy for the Overseas Territories, without going through federative solutions, later leading the parliament to approve a motion in the same direction. After that, to please the other faction, he confirmed Spínola in his post and Costa Gomes as well. The journalist ended the article by saying that nothing about this crisis appeared in the Portuguese press controlled by the regime, but that news was passing from person to person and that the whole trend of Portuguese politics in Africa was at stake.[12]

A Mirage IIIC on display at the Paris Air Show in 1961. After several expressions of interest, in 1974 Portugal finally had the budget to buy Mirage III fighters due to the financial support it received from South Africa. However, with the end of the war, the purchase did not materialise. (Keystone Press Agency)

This latest article by Bruce Loudon prompted Luís C. Lupi, from the news agency Lusitânia, to write a letter to Marcello Caetano criticising the attitude of the English journalist. In the letter, he accused Loudon of making news out of rumours and that the journalist was merely reproducing malicious gossip that aimed to hurt the President of the Council, who 'has so sacrificially put his exceptional intelligence at the service of the nation and even of those who invent the rumours'. For Lupi, the article was nothing but pure political intrigue and that Loudon 'was a paid agent of Spínola when he governed Guinea and had set up the most perfect and unfortunate machine of personal promotion that a Portuguese general ever had at his disposal.' In short, it was a 'diabolical piece of political intrigue with projection inside and outside the national walls (...)'.[13]

Meanwhile, on 12 March, Marcello Caetano met with the ministers of the military sectors. The President of the Council believed that once the National Assembly had ratified the overseas policy and the Head of State had reaffirmed his confidence – 'the competent constitutional bodies had defined the path to be followed by all the Portuguese and especially by the Armed Forces, as the instrument they should be for the execution of the policy outlined by the constituted powers'.[14] Marcello Caetano had only formalism on his side in those days, as the National Assembly did not represent the true will of the people and Américo Thomaz reappointed him because he had no other options.[15]

According to Caetano's plan, Costa Gomes and Spínola and all the generals in service in the metropolis should be asked to come before the President of the Council to say that the military 'did not have their own policy, because it was in their nature and ethics to comply with the guidelines set out by the constituted powers and that the country could be sure that they would remain on this course.' This statement was to be made by Costa Gomes with António Spínola at his side.[16] Had Caetano effectively tried to hold the generals at their post in order to keep the MFA under control or did he imagine that both would decline and sign their resignation?

In the late afternoon of 12 March, the Minister of the Army, Andrade e Silva, summoned Viana de Lemos to a meeting in the Defence Minister's office. The Secretary of State for Aeronautics was also present, and they were then informed by the Minister of Defence that it was necessary that the commands of the three branches meet in a demonstration of support and agreement with the government's overseas policy. General Andrade e Silva still said that he did not think this political manifestation was necessary, since he considered that such a manifestation might not be pleasing to the military, besides the fact that in certain meetings of the ministry, some military chiefs had already manifested themselves in favour of the overseas policy.

However, Silva Cunha insisted on the issue and as it had been agreed that the Chief of Staff, Costa Gomes, should speak at the ceremony, then he was called to the minister's office. When he was told what they wanted his role to be, he refused to take part in the ceremony.[106] He argued that he did not feel authorised to represent the military in such a demonstration because he did not know what they thought about it, but he was convinced that the Armed Forces did not agree with the procedure. Moreover, the demonstration represented an explicit support for the continuation of the war and the problem of Overseas Territories was not solved with war, but with political actions.[17] The conversation between Silva Cunha and Costa Gomes grew in tone and ended with the minister asking him if he could draw any conclusions from the decision he had taken. Costa Gomes replied yes and left the room, returning to his office.[18]

With this refusal, Costa Gomes showed that he was not aligned with overseas policy and that he was not available to take part in any kind of staging.

Later that day, on returning to his office, Costa Gomes called all the general officers who worked with him in National Defence to tell them that he was not going to take part in the demonstration in support of the government's policy. Spínola went along with him, telling him: 'I accompany you in the decision you have taken because it was the right one.'[19] Admiral Tierno Bagulho and General Ivo Ferreira of the Air Force also agreed not to participate, only Commander Peixoto Correia of the Navy disagreed with Costa Gomes. However, Ivo Ferreira would end up attending the ceremony, the only ones missing were Costa Gomes, Spínola and Tierno Bagulho. On the afternoon of 13 March, Spínola still tried to reach a consensus with Caetano by proposing that he and Costa Gomes would accept to go to the President's office with the generals who served in National Defence, but without the presence of the remaining generals of the Armed Forces.[20] But Marcello refused the proposal and the following day the ceremony took place.

On the night of the 12th to the 13th, after the meeting in the Defence Minister's office, Viana de Lemos still tried to convince Costa Gomes to change his position and that night he personally went to the general's house. The two men lived in the capital close to each other and had a close relationship. The meeting was not easy, and Costa Gomes insisted during the conversation, reported by Viana, that the Army was sick and that the government did not know how to deal with the officers, as it had gone down the path of violence, which was how he classified the transfers that had occurred. Costa Gomes showed once again that he was aware of what was happening in military circles and that the punitive measures the government had taken only aggravated the situation.

When Viana de Lemos recalled the 4 March meeting that had taken place with the commanders of the military regions to analyse the impact of Spínola's book, Costa Gomes reaffirmed that it was all a farce, since none of the generals had any authority over the military regions and some did not even know what they were doing. He also said that Marcello Caetano had offered him power, but that he did not accept because he did not want political positions. Viana de Lemos also heard Costa Gomes disqualify Andrade e Silva, who was the Minister of the Army, and accuse Silva Cunha of having Napoleonic attitudes. He also stated that if he wanted to overthrow the government, he only had to raise a finger and that deep down he even agreed with Caetano's overseas policy (which is strange given the positions he had taken) and that he had no problem in telling him that personally, but that as a group he was not available for that.[21] Viana de Lemos tried to counter-argue, but the conversation was always tense, ending at dawn. He returned home very unimpressed with Costa Gomes; after all, they had known each other for 18 years and had never had such a difficult conversation. After that night they never spoke again.

On 13 March, the head of the executive received Costa Gomes and Spínola separately and both maintained their position of not attending the ceremony scheduled for the following day, with Caetano telling them that their non-attendance would obviously imply the dismissal from their respective positions.[22] As we have already seen, Spínola also suggested, as an alternative, that he accepted to go together with Costa Gomes to Caetano's office, but separated from the remaining generals, but the proposal was not accepted.[23] From the political point of view, Caetano knew that the two generals had to appear in public to dispel any doubts about their support for the government, but it was obvious that Spínola and Costa Gomes did not want to commit themselves publicly to the policy followed until then.

The Rheumatic Brigade

On the afternoon of 14 March, the audience was held with the generals of the Army, Navy, Air Force and Security Forces, who were present in large numbers in the main hall of São Bento Palace.[24] Due to Costa Gomes's refusal to attend, the Army Chief of Staff, General Paiva Brandão, was invited to speak, as he was the oldest of the Chiefs of Staff. The ceremony would become known as the meeting of the rheumatic brigade, due to the age of the generals present, and would be broadcasted by radio and television.[25]

Paiva Brandão stated in his speech, which was previously outlined by the President of the Council, that:

> ... the Armed Forces do not conduct politics, but it is their imperative duty, and also our ethics, to accomplish the mission that has been determined for us by the legally constituted Government. Throughout our history, of more than eight centuries, it has been the unity of the Portuguese, even in the most critical occasions, that has awakened the necessary courage and confidence to follow the most appropriate course in the national interest. This affirmation of unity is also the reason for our presence.

Brandão then alluded to the President of the Council's speech on 5 March, stating that 'it will never be too much to remember that the military operations in Angola, Mozambique and Guinea resulted from legitimate defence in the face of aggression prepared and unleashed from foreign territories.' Brandão went on to say that when the collective interest, such as the protection of populations that continued to be threatened, demanded that the defence effort be continued, in search of a peace based on justice and progress, above all the Armed Forces wanted to 'remain united and solidary.' And he ended by saying that 'at a time when the progress of the nation and the well-being of the Portuguese depend on the protection given to them by the military forces, it is also appropriate to tell Your Excellency [President of the Council] that we are united, firm and will do our duty whenever and wherever the national interest demands it.'

For his part, the head of government said that he had listened and accepted the statement of 'loyalty and discipline' of the Armed Forces and stressed 'that the Armed Forces not only cannot have any other policy that is not the one defined by the constituted powers of the Republic, but they are, and have to be with that policy when it is the defence of national integrity.' Caetano ended by saying that 'the country is sure that it can count on its Armed Forces. At all levels there can be no doubt about the attitude of its commanders.'[26] In fact, the commanders were there showing their loyalty, the problem was that they no longer represented the captains.

The speeches at the demonstration were widely disseminated in the written press. On 15 March, the front page of the *Diário Popular* headlined: 'High ranking officers of the Armed Forces express their support to the Government's action' and inside it wrote, quoting Caetano: 'the country is sure that it can count on the Armed Forces,' developing that dozens of general officers of the three branches of the Armed Forces were present, including the commanders of the military regions of the continent and those of the security corporations also came to São Bento to state their support for Marcello Caetano.[27]

Meanwhile, Costa Gomes and Spínola were dismissed that day and the President of the Council immediately appointed General Luz Cunha, who was commander-in-chief in Angola and had held the post of Army Minister, to the post of Chief of General Staff of the Armed Forces.[28] Another name that was considered was that of Bettencourt Rodrigues, but due to the short time he had been in command in Guinea and the difficulty in replacing him, he was

Portuguese General Joaquim Da Luz Cunha who was named Chief of Staff of the Armed Forces on 14 March. Luz Cunha was a strong defender of the Portuguese presence in Africa and was linked to the most conservative sectors of the regime. His appointment left the captains even more dissatisfied. (AP)

The Minister of the Army, General Andrade e Silva, greets Marcello Caetano after the vote of confidence given to the government by the regime's generals. (Miranda Castela collection/Archive of the Assembly of the Republic)

Marcello Caetano (left) and Rui Patrício (right). It seems that in the final phase of the regime, Caetano even thought of him as a possible head of the executive. (Bill Beck collection)

not chosen.[29] As for Spínola's position, it was not filled and was eventually suppressed.

However, Caetano felt insecure about the decision he had taken and despondent about what was happening around him, as testified by Elmano Alves, a member of parliament in the National Assembly. On that Friday, 14 April, the deputy found the head of the government very depressed with the whole situation he had experienced. Caetano confessed that he was tired and ill and that he had already asked the President of the Republic to replace him, suggesting Baltazar Rebello de Sousa, Minister of Overseas Territories or Rui Patrício, Minister of Foreign Affairs, to take his place.[30]

Regarding the process that led to the dismissal of the two generals, the President of the Republic would later take a rather critical stance towards the actions of the head of government. For Américo Thomaz, what had happened was that, once again, Marcello Caetano did not have the courage to proceed with the dismissal in a frontal manner. For the Head of State, this attitude was yet another mistake and, above all, a sign of weakness. He also suspected that the demonstration in support of the Government's policy was organised to avoid the dismissal of the two generals, since if they had attended, they would certainly not have been dismissed.[31]

The Admiral also complained about the way found by the President of the Council to solve the issue, since it was not previously communicated to Belém and did not meet with the approval of the Head of State. Thomaz recalls that he was informed of the demonstration by two general officers who wanted to explain to him the reason for their non-attendance.[32] For the President of the Republic, the demonstration accentuated 'the split in the officer corps into two parts, that of the hierarchy and that of the rest.'

In relation to Paiva Brandão's speech, which ended with the affirmation of unity in the Armed Forces, Thomaz would comment that 'union did not exist in fact, as the officialdom of the three branches of the Armed Forces was split into two parts, comprising the already senior officers and the younger officers, strongly disconnected from their chiefs, who had, in fact, ceased to exercise any action over them.'[33]

On 15 March, the dismissal of the two generals was the subject of a telegram from the French ambassador in Lisbon to Paris, saying that this put an end to a dangerous, even intolerable, situation for the prestige and stability of the government. In his opinion, Caetano could no longer accept that two generals openly opposed to his overseas policy should remain in the highest ranks of the military hierarchy. However, he considered that this measure did not mean that there was Army cohesion, given that the exoneration of Spínola would increase the resentment of the intermediate military cadres, among whom General Spínola's prestige was great. 'As far as we know, the climate of unrest, which has other causes, has been maintained in recent days among the captains and commanders, the authorities consider, however, that they may have taken a calculated risk, since the state of alert proclaimed yesterday has already been lifted.' The diplomat concluded this telegram by stating that regardless of the internal repercussions, the Spínola case could only further weaken Portugal's position in international forums, increase foreign pressure for a modification of its policy in Africa and strengthen the confidence of the liberation movements in their success.[34]

Government Reshuffle

When he was received by Américo Thomaz on 11 March, Caetano addressed the President of the Republic, saying that what concerned him was to continue with government activity and he was particularly attentive to the economic situation, exemplifying this with the worsening inflation resulting from the oil crisis at the end of the previous year. In his memoirs he writes that the country had, for:

> … quite a few years, a positive annual balance of international payments which allowed it to conserve and increase its gold and foreign currency reserves. But the increase in the price of crude oil to be imported was in itself equivalent to the annual balance as it had been the year before. The implications of higher energy prices on the cost of other products were inevitable. With these arguments Marcello justified the need to reorganize the government's economic sector immediately after Carnaval, but the 'incident' of the publication of Spínola's book led him to suspend the reshuffle.

However, Marcello gave the idea of maintaining the urgency of the reshuffle by stating that it should not be delayed any longer. Caetano also explained to Thomaz the general outline of the changes to be made: the separation of Finance and Economy, as he felt it was too much for one man to bear, and the splitting of the Economy into two ministries: one for Agriculture and Commerce,

Manuel Cotta Dias (in the centre) was Caetano's minister for two years until the end of the regime. He was in charge of Finance and the Economy, which were later separated into two different departments in the March 1974 reshuffle. (DGARQ-CFP-SNI)

the other for Industry and Energy. However, at this meeting on 11 March, Caetano noted that the President of the Republic seemed to him 'not in a very good mood' and he remarked on all the organic and personnel solutions he had formulated, as well as the priorities for action he had indicated, being more concerned with the impact of Spínola's book, as we have seen above. Thomaz clearly showed his displeasure with the situation.[35] However, Caetano would go ahead with his intentions and on 14 March the new government took office.

In a document from March, but without a precise date, Marcello Caetano's personal archive contains a speech addressed to ministers, secretaries of state and under-secretaries of state strictly for economic affairs and in which he explains the economic reorganisation, stating that 'it is very much about one person' keeping the ministries of Economy and Finance. At the time, the Ministry of Finance and Economy was headed by Manuel Cotta Dias, a man from the regime, who had held various management positions over time and had been a minister since 1972.

At the end of his speech, also delivered at São Bento Palace, he stated that the Government was 'fighting on many fronts', revealing that these fronts were 'beset by obstacles' that were appearing independently of his will and often without the possibility of foreseeing them. Just one day after the demonstration of support by the military hierarchy in that same place, he admits before a new audience: 'I really don't know if the nation has ever faced so many adversaries simultaneously, due to the enmity of men, others due to the adversity of circumstances. But faced with the gravity and multiplicity of the struggles to be sustained, we cannot fold our arms. We must respond to every challenge. We are here to fight'. In a somewhat contradictory and premonitory attitude, he ends once again without explaining what he is referring to specifically: 'Victory may or may not come if it does not depend only on us. But in all cases, we are left with the consciousness of duty done. And the truth is that I have faith in our capacity to overcome adverse fates.'[36]

During these days, the French ambassador in Lisbon, Bernard Durand, showed himself well informed and was busy writing correspondence; it was only on 13 March that he sent a five-page letter entitled 'L'affaire Spínola' and a telegram on the situation in Portugal to the French Ministry of Foreign Affairs.

In the first, Durand began by saying that the turmoil caused by the book had been appeased, at least temporarily, because other consequences were inevitable in the more or less long term, and he considered it useful to return to this case 'without precedent in the history of the Estado Novo.'

The reaction of conservative circles was not long in coming and they resorted to their usual representative, Thomaz, to put an end to a dangerous situation. For the conservatives, 'more salazarist than Salazar', any slowing down of the war effort or any weakening of the powers of central power was reprehensible. The ambassador believed that it was because of Thomaz, the ultras and those with vested interests that Caetano made exceptional use of communication in the National Assembly to proclaim the continuation of the policy. A confidence motion was drafted under the control of Marcello Caetano himself. The diplomat noted that eight days after this intervention in parliament and three weeks after the publication of the book, Spínola remained discreet in his post. A situation that 'shows the singular and tortuous nature of the customs of this country, but also the risks that the sacking of a general officer seen as a triumphant in the past can represent for power.' However, he was of the opinion that the authority of the State could not allow this situation to continue for long.[37]

As for the reshuffle in the governing cast, it was viewed with surprise by the French ambassador in Lisbon who, in a telegram on 13 March about the situation in Portugal, began by referring to a meeting of the Council of Ministers on the 12th in which a review of the Ministries of Economy was decided. And it went on to say, against all the odds, no measures seemed to have been taken to end the crisis dividing the Army and public opinion after Spínola's position in the book. Although in conflict with his government over overseas policy, the second figure in the Portuguese Army remained in office for the time being.

Caetano, who had satisfied the extreme right by reaffirming the broad lines of his African policy, hesitated to sanction the general for fear of the reactions that such a decision would provoke in the army, Durand noted. The division in the army was a worrying aspect of the

Costa Gomes and Spínola were clearly on a collision course with Marcello Caetano in 1974. After the military coup they would be among the most important figures of the new regime. (Flama archive)

situation and, in the diplomat's opinion, explained the President of the Council's hesitation, since the military forces, together with the police, were the regime's main support, and the pursuit of its policies in Africa depended on them.[38]

In the US, the CIA (Central Intelligence Agency) also produced information on the situation in Portugal. On 15 March, the agency reported that the dismissal of Costa Gomes and Spínola represented 'a victory for the right-wing forces' that were against Spínola's ideas of greater autonomy for the African colonies. In the Agency's view it was likely that the dismissal of the two generals would cause shock waves 'throughout the Portuguese hierarchy, including many supporters of Spínola' and that the government, anticipating this, had reinstated the state of alert that confined 'troops to barracks for four days this week.' The CIA also had indications that the name chosen to replace Costa Gomes as Chief of Staff was Luz Cunha, who had commanded the Portuguese forces in Angola since 1972, and that Spínola's post would remain vacant. Finally, the Agency reported that over the past week the government had placed military personnel sympathetic to Spínola in locations as far away from Lisbon as possible. In this sense, the American consulate in the Azores had reported rumours of the arrival in the Azores of 48 officers, probably officers who, like Spínola, supported a change in Portuguese overseas policy.[39]

Freitas do Amaral, a former student and collaborator of Marcello Caetano, says in his memoirs about the last ministerial reshuffle, which took place on the eve of the Caldas da Rainha revolt, that he worked on it for over a year and that it was based on a study made by a commission he chaired. Freitas states that it was not just a change of people but a reorganisation of the various economic ministries along the lines of the solutions adopted in France and England. And he exemplified this with the creation of a large Ministry of Finance and Economic Coordination, as well as the extinction of the Ministry of Economy and the creation, in its place, of two important sectorial ministries: the Ministry of Agriculture and the Ministry of Industry. Freitas do Amaral states that the only point on which Marcello did not agree with his project was the one regarding the location of the department in charge of Commerce (Marcello had exonerated the former Secretary of State for Commerce). While Freitas proposed an integrated Secretary of State in the Ministry of Finance, to better articulate the fight against inflation, Caetano decided to join it to Agriculture, a department which was renamed Ministry of Agriculture and Commerce.[40]

2
THE FIRST REBELLION

The dismissal of Costa Gomes and Spínola aggravated the unease in the Armed Forces. The MFA members felt the situation was a provocation, and the appointment of General Luz Cunha as CEMGFA was seen as a surrender by Marcello to the regime's hard-line.[1] Luz Cunha had allegedly been involved with General Kaúlza de Arriaga (also supported by Silvino Silvério Marques and Henrique Troni) in an attempted coup against Marcello Caetano in December 1973. The intention would be denounced by the movement of the captains, nullifying any move by Arriaga. When confronted directly by Marcello Caetano, on 19 December 1973, Kaúlza denied that he was preparing a coup, although he had told the President of the Council that he thought it was urgent to change the government.[2]

The departure of Costa Gomes and Spínola had caused instability in the Armed Forces and the first signs of this occurred in Caldas da Rainha. Already on 12 March, several officers in that unit had told the acting commander, Lieutenant Colonel Farinha Tavares, that if anything happened to Costa Gomes and Spínola they would take a position of force.[3] The dissatisfaction also reached the north of the country to the special operations training centre in Lamego (CIOE, *Centro de Instrução de Operações Especiais*, Special Operations Troops Centre), where several officers protested against the dismissal of the two top leaders of the Armed Forces. The unit commander, Colonel Amílcar Alves, and the second in command, Major Nelson Valente, pretended to be on the side of the protesting military in order to later promote, together with the commanders of the North Military Region, the transfer to other units of the captains that had contested the government's decision.[4] However, on 15 March, the atmosphere in Lamego was one of insurrection and several officers from the CIOE did not accept the dismissal of Costa Gomes and Spínola. José Monteiro Valente, who was at the time a captain in Lamego, recounts that on the morning of 15 March, several captains expressed to the unit commander their dissatisfaction with the dismissal of the two generals and the loss of confidence in the commander of the Northern Military Region, who had participated in Lisbon in the ceremony of loyalty to the government. The captains were angry, but for the moment they did not want to take forceful action. However, that day, rumours appeared in other units that Lamego had revolted and that the troops of the CIOE were available to leave and march towards Lisbon.[5]

These rumours reached the Viseu Infantry Regiment (RI14), in the centre of the country, where there was also dissatisfaction. On the afternoon of the 15th, several captains of this unit declared that they did not agree with the dismissal of the two generals and that they were from that moment on under the orders of Spínola and Costa Gomes. This position was communicated to the unit commander, Colonel José Augusto Sá Cardoso, who did not oppose the position taken.[6] In the northern region, other officers linked to the MFA expressed their support to their colleagues in Lamego and protested

Kaúlza de Arriaga at lunch with Spínola and other generals. Arriaga was one of the regime's best-known generals and connected to right-wing circles. He was a strong advocate of Portugal staying in Africa and even conspired against Marcello Caetano, but without success. (António de Spínola collection)

The city of Lamego in the 70s with the castle on top of the hill. It was in this city that the training centre for special troops (CIOE) was located. (José Matos collection)

had been circulating for several days that Costa Gomes and Spínola might be dismissed, and some officers did not accept such a decision willingly. In Caldas, the most active were Lieutenant Vítor Carvalho and Captain Virgílio Varela, who, on the night of 14–15 March, secretly went to Lisbon, to the house of Major Casanova Ferreira, to demand that the MFA take a strong stance in the face of the imminent dismissal of the two generals. The two representatives of the commission of militia officers knew that Casanova Ferreira had participated in the elaboration of an order of operations, which had been suspended due to the lack of conditions to carry out the coup. This order had been prepared in view of the possibility of carrying out the coup on 14 March, to avoid the dismissal of Costa Gomes and Spínola, and to make the ceremony of the generals in São Bento unfeasible. For this purpose, several officers of the movement met on the morning of 12 March, at Casanova Ferreira's house, to prepare an action in force and combine the contacts to be made.

Thus, on the morning of the 13th, Otelo went to Santarém with the operations order to the commanders of their respective units. A general climate of protest thus began to emerge, with consequences at various levels.[7]

In Lisbon, on the night of 15–16 March, some MFA officers, such as Otelo, Manuel Monge, Armando Marques Ramos, and Casanova Ferreira, noticed the unrest in Caldas da Rainha and Lamego and noted the willingness of these two units to go out to the streets and take up a position of strength. However, the MFA was not yet in a position to support a military revolt, given that there was not yet a definitive order of operations, nor a political programme.

In Caldas da Rainha, the officers of the Regiment of Infantry 5 (RI5) were restless and prepared for any action. The movements in Caldas had even led to a visit, in early March, by Brigadier Pedro Serrano, second-in-command of the Tomar Military Region. Farinha Tavares, who commanded the unit, became aware of the subversive positions of the regiment's officers. On 9 March, they showed solidarity with the military prisoners; on 12 March, they went, one by one, to the interim commander to show support for generals Costa Gomes and Spínola, who were going to be dismissed for not attending the demonstration in support of the government's policy.

On 13 March, the regiment was again visited by Brigadier Pedro Serrano, making the officers of RI5 even more uneasy.[8] Information and attended a meeting at the home of Captain Joaquim Manuel Correia Bernardo, where several officers of the EPC (*Escola Prática de Cavalaria*, Cavalry Practical School) were present but did not convince the young lieutenants and captains of the possibility of launching armed action the next day. Still on the afternoon of that day, Otelo took part in a wider meeting with the EPC officers and paratroopers from the Tancos base, who had been summoned to the meeting. Both considered that the document had no substance. The paratroopers demanded a well-defined operations plan and the guaranteed adhesion of units considered to be fundamental. At a later meeting, in Lisbon, they themselves assumed that they would present a plan within 10 days and that they had a combat force of approximately 800 men, which could be the main force to overthrow the regime. However, they needed the support of other units, which would be guaranteed by the MFA.[9] Otelo thus concluded that the plan they hastily put together lacked strength and structure of any kind. The attempt to implement it would also not save the two generals from dismissal and the plan was abandoned, leaving the movement waiting for an eventual action by the paratroopers, which would then be supported by the MFA.[10]

But at the imminence of the dismissal of the two generals, Vítor Carvalho and Virgílio Varela decide to contact Casanova Ferreira for the movement to do something. Casanova managed to dissuade Varela from participating in a rash move with the promise that he would resume the plan of operations to improve it. Nevertheless, Varela said he would keep the forces he had in RI5 in a state of readiness. His 'willingness to leave' also had to do with the fact that on Monday, 19 March, the soldiers from the course of sergeant-militiamen who were at the end of their conscription were going to do a field week, where they would stay for one to two weeks, and that it would not be possible to count on them. The captain argued that it was important to act at that moment. Varela was also concerned about his professional situation in the Armed Forces. As he was a militia captain, he did not have great prospects of becoming a permanent officer, after the revocation of Decrees nos. 353/73 and 409/73, and Spínola, as Vice-CEMGFA (*Vice-Chefe do Estado-Maior General das Forças Armadas*, Vice-Chief of Staff of the Armed Forces), had promised to solve the problem of the militiamen, who did not advance beyond the rank of captain. He therefore felt that he had to act and that the most that could happen to him was to be arrested, a problem that he minimised to a certain extent. For him, the PIDE/DGS (*Polícia Internacional e de Defesa do Estado/Direcção Geral de Segurança*, International and State Defence Police/Directorate General for Security) was not a threat, as he was convinced that they would not interfere with the military, having information that there were agents of the DGS collaborating with the movement (which was not true), but which in Varela's perception made sense considering that, in Africa, the military often worked in collaboration with the DGS in the collection of information.[11] After their conversation with Casanova Ferreira, the two officers returned to Caldas da Rainha at dawn and heard on the car radio the news of Marcello Caetano's dispatch announcing the dismissal of Costa Gomes and Spínola and they decided to act as soon as possible.[12]

One day after being dismissed, Spínola had lunch in Lisbon with the military close to him: Alcino Ribeiro, Rafael Durão, Almeida

The 5th Infantry Regiment in Caldas da Rainha, where the first military revolt against the regime broke out in March 1974. (*Diário de Notícias*)

Portuguese paratroopers in training. In 1974, the paratroopers were among the most powerful forces in the country and for the MFA it was important that they remained neutral and did not interfere in operations to overthrow the regime. (NATO collection)

Bruno, Dias de Lima, and António Ramos. Spínola was informed of the prevailing climate and considered that this would not be 'the right moment to take any action' since the government 'should remain on alert for the time being and that, therefore, we should enter into a phase of apparent calm, taking advantage of this period to complete the planning and ensure a perfect coordination of the action to be launched in due course.'[13]

Aware of the unrest in Caldas, Otelo and Casanova were determined to meet on the 15th and draw up an operations plan. They knocked on Manuel Monge's door to arrange a working meeting for 08:00 am the next day, but shortly afterwards Armando Marques Ramos joined them, visibly worried. Armando Ramos confirmed that on the 12th several RI5 officers had told the commander that if anything happened to the two generals 'there would be trouble,' as they would take an active position. With the announced dismissal 'they consider that their word is at stake, and they want to come out to the street.' Armando Ramos said that he wanted to go to Caldas to try to calm the unit down and received a message from Casanova: 'we were precisely arranging a meeting with Monge for tomorrow at 08:00 am to cook up a proper operations plan. You can tell that to the guys in Caldas. Tell them to be calm because we are working.'

According to Otelo, it was around 09:00 pm when the phone rang. A call from the CIOE in Lamego, from Captain Manuel Ferreira da Silva, telling him that they had not accepted the order from the Northern Military Region to transfer the commander to Espinho, after he had apparently shown solidarity with the Lamego officers who had protested against the dismissal of the two generals. Manuel Monge, who had answered the phone, reported that Lamego was in rebellion and that they were going to pull out of the barracks 'all over the place.'[14]

This confusing telephone call, which helped light the fuse of 16 March, was later explained in a letter by Manuel Ferreira da Silva:

On the 15th, at night, I telephoned Major Manuel Monge at his house (we had been together in Gadamael, during the critical phase in Guinea, in 1973) communicating to him the position taken and that we were waiting for any instructions from the movement, because at that moment it would be possible to go out to the streets with troops.

After this phone call, and since there was no order from the movement to leave, Ferreira da Silva went to bed.[15] The captain also explained that on the 14th, at night, the captains of the CIOE of Lamego (about 15) met and expressed their displeasure with the situation and resolved that on the following day they would communicate to the commander their solidarity with the generals referred to and their non-acceptance of the channel of command of the Northern Military Region. On the following day, in the morning, the captains gathered near the commander's office and meanwhile communicated what had been decided the day before (the spokesman was Captain Bordalo, being the oldest). After the position was taken, the officers carried out several actions that translated into the clarification of the graduates about the position taken. The reaction was positive, but no instructions were given for eventual exits from the unit. In the afternoon, Ferreira da Silva and the other officers contacted other units about the position taken. In general, these units listened, but were not very enthusiastic. Lieutenant Colonel Carlos Azeredo, from CICA 1 (Auto 1 Instruction and Driving Centre) in Porto, and officers from RI 14 (Viseu's Infantry Regiment), who said they would transmit a similar position to their command.[16]

On the morning of the 16th, the officers from Lamego learned about the action from Caldas da Rainha through the radio. 'Only in the afternoon of that day 16, we received a communication from Caldas, stating that they were surrounded, asking for our support.' At that time, the 2nd commander of CIOE had already mobilised some sergeants against the attitude of the officers, says the letter. However, the occurrence of an accident during instruction, caused by the accidental detonation of a grenade, which caused two deaths and some serious injuries, evacuated by helicopter, also contributed to cool the spirits of the unit.[17]

Ferreira da Silva concluded that 'the attitude of the captains was solely of their own initiative and totally unconnected to the movement.' Their initial attitude was not to take to the streets, but to make a stand. The telephone call he made to Manuel Monge, 'although it may have precipitated March 16, was only to alert them to our position. The departure from Caldas was on your initiative and without the knowledge of the CIOE. On 15 and 16 March there were forces in a position to leave if requested.'[18]

Another captain from Lamego, Bordalo Xavier, said that on 15 March, the captains assigned to the movement had been waiting to receive orders to leave with troops. He also said that, on the night of that day, he received a phone call from Caldas da Rainha asking if those at Lamego had already left, which perplexed him as no order to leave had reached Lamego.[19]

Back at Manuel Monge's house, he had a plan of operations right there with him and it was decided to recover it and redistribute objectives. Armando Marques Ramos would proceed to Caldas and gave instructions to arrest the unit commanders, if they did not join, they would march to Lisbon with a motorised column and one or two companies, meet in Espinheira with a column from the EPC at Santarém and once in Lisbon, take over Portela airport. Captain Ramos took some notes of these instructions and left for Caldas. Monge would wait at the roundabout of the statue of St Christopher, next to the Light Artillery Regiment 1, for the columns coming from the north to give them missions. In addition to this function, Monge would take charge through personal and telephone contact to try to persuade other units that could immediately join the revolt. Casanova Ferreira would go to Santarém to the EPC, in order to bring with him to Lisbon a squadron of armoured vehicles, to face any attempt of resistance from the forces loyal to the government. Otelo Saraiva de Carvalho would call at Vendas Novas (Artillery Practical School) to order a battery of howitzers to perform bombardment actions in lieu of the Air Force and would follow with Germano Miquelina Simões to the EPI (*Escola Prática de Infantaria*, Infantry Practical School) of Mafra to bring from there a company to assault and control *Rádio Clube Português*. Otelo mentions in his description of events that he objected to the plan because it was the weekend and many soldiers had gone home on leave and there were a number of other problems that were not properly solved, but Casanova Ferreira insisted that all it needed was a shake-up for the regime to fall. Otelo, despite his reservations, did not want to appear weak and sided with Monge and Casanova.[20] He said goodbye to his two colleagues at 9:30 p.m. and would only see them again on 25 April.[21]

After each went their separate ways, Monge went to the Military Academy, where a party of Engineering cadets were, to speak with Lieutenant Colonel Almeida Bruno to prevent the paratroopers from taking any action against the movement. Monge was suspicious of the commitment of the paratroopers to a military revolt and had to ensure that they would not have a hostile attitude if the coup was led by the Army. Almeida Bruno was one of Spínola's trusted men and was with the MFA and knew, together with Monge, two officers with great prestige among the paratroopers: Lieutenant Colonel Mensurado and Colonel Rafael Durão, who had also been in Guinea. Monge reports that they spoke with Durão and 'we asked them not to let the paratroopers come out against us,' but while they were in the Academy, they realised that GNR (*Guarda Nacional Republicana*, National Republican Guard) forces were surrounding that institution and they left quickly so as not to be arrested.[22] After having escaped the GNR siege, they went to Spínola's house to inform him personally of what was happening. Major Jaime Neves, who had also been at the meeting at the Academy, was also at the meeting in Spínola's house. They informed Spínola of the great agitation in some military units in the north of the country, with the Lamego special forces about to advance to Lisbon. The three

Otelo entered the Caldas revolt with reservations but did everything in his power to make the coup work. Luckily, he was neither arrested nor detected by the political police. (AFP)

officers argued that units in the south of the country assigned to the MFA should be activated to support the uprising in the north. Spínola did not discourage them and told them that Costa Gomes had told him they could count on Colonel António Romeiras Júnior – commander of Cavalry Regiment 7 (RC 7) – in Lisbon, in case Costa Gomes needed protection.[23] According to Spínola, Colonel Romeiras was 'two hundred per cent' with Costa Gomes, 'so they could openly count on his collaboration.'[24] Monge was suspicious of this collaboration, since he knew that Romeiras was the brother-in-law of Viana de Lemos, the Under-Secretary of State for the Army, but Spínola insisted that they could count on Romeiras.[25]

By chance, that same night, Romeiras had been having dinner with Viana de Lemos and shortly after midnight they were warned by the Army Minister, Andrade e Silva, of military movements in the north of the country, especially in Lamego. In view of the situation, the minister ordered all the units to be on strict guard and Viana de Lemos went immediately to the Ministry of Defence, while António Romeiras went to RC 7, where shortly after arriving he received a visit from Monge and Jaime Neves with a very strange request.[26] They wanted Romeiras to send a military escort to General Costa Gomes' house and bring him to the barracks, as his life was in danger. Romeiras refuses the request arguing that the general was in no danger and immediately afterwards called Viana de Lemos to report what had happened.[27] Obviously, both Monge and Jaime Neves were referenced, and that same night PIDE/DGS went to their house to arrest and interrogate them, although they were not at home.[28] In his memoirs, Viana de Lemos denied that it was him or the Army Minister who ordered the political police to act against these officers. He did not know who gave the order,[29] but the order seems to have come from military circles. Óscar Cardoso, who was a deputy inspector of the DGS, tells that on that night he received orders from the military to go to Miraflores to arrest Manuel Monge, having gone to the house of this officer with two other agents of the political police. After searching the house, Monge was nowhere to be found.[30]

During the night, Otelo was busy making contacts to mobilise other units that could participate in the coup. By phone or in person, Otelo contacted several officers who were committed to the captains' movement, but he could not get the support he needed. This was the case with the EPA (*Escola Prática de Artilharia*, Artillery Practical School) in Vendas Novas, where Otelo called to ask for an artillery battery for Lisbon. On the other end of the line, he heard the captain,

After the revolution, Jaime Neves led the Amadora Commando regiment, one of the military units that put an end to the influence of the radical military left in Portugal. Jaime Neves was involved in the 16 March uprising and also in the 25 April revolution. (AEI)

who was the day officer, tell him that at that time not even a platoon could be arranged to go to Lisbon, let alone a battery. All the men had left for the weekend. Otelo then left for Mafra with Miquelina Simões as agreed, where they arrived at 03:00 am in the morning. When they arrived at the EPI, they were informed that the unit had gone into strict lockdown two hours ago, so it would not be possible to leave.[31] It was a sign that the authorities in Lisbon were already aware of the situation and, as we have seen, it was the Army Minister himself who had decreed strict prevention.

Earlier, around 11:00 pm, Armando Marques Ramos arrived in Caldas da Rainha and presented himself at the barracks as the bearer of orders for a motorised column to march to the capital. Ramos met with the Caldas officers to decide who would command the column and none of the captains present wanted to assume this responsibility. It was then decided that Marques Ramos would be together with Captain Victor Carvalho to command the column.[32] One of the men of the RI5, Captain Gonçalves Novo, spoke of two meetings that night, the first to choose freely the captain who would command operations and a second in which Marques Ramos was chosen to command the column of the regiment that would follow to Lisbon to take the airport.[33] However, this version is not agreed upon among the protagonists of the revolt. Adelino de Matos Coelho, who was a lieutenant at the time, argues that the commander of the column was Captain Luís Piedade Faria, as he was the commander of the main force that was mobilised to head for Lisbon. Moreover, in the conclusions of the enquiry that was set up regarding the Caldas revolt, it is clearly stated that it was Captain Piedade Faria who led an armed column from Caldas, basically made up of the company of which he was commander, 'to whose elements he gave orders and instructions, on its way to Lisbon.'[34] Thus, it seems to have been Luís Piedade Faria who took command of the column, although Marques Ramos argues that at the decisive meeting that night no officer from the unit was available to take command of the rebellious troops.

This first coup attempt was neutralised by the government forces, although there was no confrontation, as the Caldas troops retreated when they saw they were alone. In this photo we can see a column of vehicles from the 15th Infantry Regiment from Tomar, stationed close to the uprising unit during siege operations. (*Diário de Notícias*)

The 1st Air Region Command was located at the top of Monsanto Forest Park in Lisbon, and it was here that the government sought refuge on 16 March 1974. (National Defence archive)

crossed the barrack gates in the direction of the capital the government was already on high alert and prepared to face the rebellious soldiers. The column that left the barracks was made up of 13 vehicles, and it was not possible to determine the exact number of soldiers involved in the revolt, but it was thought to be around 180 men.[35]

Besides leaving Caldas and despite the steps taken, no other military force left that night and the officers of RI5 advanced alone towards the capital, convinced that they were not the only ones. They still thought they would find an armoured column coming from the EPC in Santarém, but nothing happened. Three kilometres from the capital they were informed by Monge and Casanova, who went to meet them, that the coup had failed and that no one else had joined the military uprising. Casanova had also failed to convince the soldiers in Santarém to leave the barracks. In short, no unit had left, not even from Lamego, and in Lisbon the forces loyal to the regime were waiting for the Caldas column.[36] Thus, they were forced to retreat and Monge and Casanova accompanied the column back to Caldas da Rainha, where they intended to resist.[37]

At home, Marcello Caetano was getting ready for bed when he received a phone call from the Minister of Defence warning about the military unrest in some of the country's barracks. Marcello did not go to bed that night and stayed attentive by the phone waiting for further news, when he received information that military forces from Caldas da Rainha had left the barracks in the direction of Lisbon. It was then, around 03:00 in the morning, that Caetano decided to leave home accompanied by his military adjutant, heading to the headquarters of the 1st Airborne Region, in the Monsanto Forest Park (Lisbon).[38] It was in that barracks that Caetano would seek refuge in case of emergency, as it was there that he would be able to coordinate the government's reaction. He stayed in Monsanto for the rest of the night, accompanied by the Minister of the Navy and the Secretary of State for Aeronautics and in contact with the ministers of Defence and of the Army who were in Terreiro do Paço.[39]

Convinced that the movement had triggered a military coup, the officers involved decided to neutralise the commander. The new commander, Colonel Horácio Lopes Rodrigues, had taken office the day before and was surprised that night in his office, together with the second commander, Lieutenant Colonel Farinha Tavares, by the insurgent officers. Captain Luz Varela and Lieutenant Silva Carvalho entered the office with pistols in hand and invited the two commanders to join the coup. As they refused, they were detained in the office, but the insurgents made the mistake of not removing the commander's private telephone from the office. As soon as he could, Lopes Rodrigues called Lisbon and Tomar and sounded the alert. When at 04:00 am in the morning of 16 March, the column

As Caetano summarised, the reaction to the military uprising was conducted from the Army Ministry in order to intercept the military force coming from Caldas. The forces loyal to the government waited for the column at the entrance to Lisbon, but, as we have seen, the military rebels were warned that no other unit had joined the coup and ended up reversing their march, returning to their point of origin.

On the events of 16 March, the President of the Republic linked Spínola's dismissal to the Caldas da Rainha uprising, since it took place less than two days after his dismissal and the main participants were officers loyal to the general. Thomaz confesses that he does not know if the movement had military support in Lisbon, but if it did, they did not manifest themselves. In his notes on the event, Américo Thomaz recalls, years later, that he was woken up at one o'clock in the morning, 'on the night of the 15th to the 16th, because telephone conversations were detected, which indicated the possible outbreak of military insubordination.' The Admiral says that he spent the night in silence and went, around six o'clock in the morning, to the Monsanto barracks, where Marcello Caetano was already. During his stay in Monsanto, Thomaz says he did not appreciate 'the atmosphere' he found, referring to the lack of interest, at least apparent:

> I only found the Army Minister truly diligent, hard-working and determined. In the President of the Council, I noticed a detachment, which seemed to me almost total, and which really shocked me: in short and in conclusion, I did not return home well impressed, nor optimistic. [...] I was bothered by the passivity and the almost general detachment, which did not seem to me a good omen.[40]

The involvement of Spínola is also pointed out by the Minister of Defence, Silva Cunha, in a letter he wrote a few days later to the military commander of Guinea, General Bettencourt Rodrigues. In this letter, Silva Cunha expressed to Rodrigues his concerns about the political situation in the mainland, which had worsened with the publication of Spínola's book and the consequent exoneration of the two generals. The situation had caused discontent in the military ranks and led to the Caldas military revolt. The minister said that the government had acted 'quickly and efficiently,' but he recognised 'that there were wounds that needed to be healed, some requiring drastic treatment,' and he did not know whether there would not be another 'explosion of discontent' in the future. However, he was convinced that Spínola 'had no part in the events but had the memory of the book and the atmosphere it created.' He ended the letter by regretting that, 'when there is so much to do in favour of the Armed Forces, he has to waste time on security issues, but it is necessary to install discipline and the country's confidence in its troops.'[41]

Present at the Army General Staff during the Caldas revolt, General Silvino Silvério Marques found, years later, that when he was asked by the Army Chief of Staff to explain and justify to the most senior officers and those present in the offices what was happening, they listened in silence. 'To his astonishment, he found out that almost all of them were MFA officers.'[42] This was a game of shadows: many military personnel were only apparently on the side of the regime's forces.

The confusion generated by the lack of coordination between the elements of the movement on the night of 15–16 March was mirrored in an article sent to the preliminary examination commission by the daily *Jornal do Comércio*, to be published on the 17th. Entitled 'Hours of expectation (before the official communiqué) in a life without jolts,' the extensive article began by noting that 'the most unconnected rumours were simmering in Lisbon,' while the population was not receiving official news of what was happening. There was talk of military movements in various parts of the country. This part of the article was censored. The news reported, and the previous examining commission had it cut, that at 02:00 am a detachment of the GNR surrounded the Military Academy, where a meeting of the ringleaders of a military attempt was to take place. Without confirmed information, the newspaper wanted to advance that there was talk of arrests and that a military column had left from Lamego at dawn and would have been joined by other elements in Viseu and that advanced to Caldas da Rainha, joining the forces stationed there. From that city they continued, approaching Lisbon, then retreating to Caldas in view of the defence that had been established in the capital. The newspaper had confirmed on a tour of the various barracks of the PSP (*Polícia de Segurança Pública*, Public Security Police) and GNR that in all units maintained strict precautions. The daily also reported that the situation had led to a meeting in National Defence of the respective minister, the Minister of the Navy, the Minister of the Army and the Under-Secretary of State for the Army.

The entrances to the city had been cordoned off at dawn by military detachments, namely armoured and parachute forces, backed up by PSP shock companies, with special focus on the eastern part of the city, Portela airport, Moscavide and Sacavém. All the units and military establishments that were in a state of alert had changed to a state of strict prevention. The news also mentions that about 14 FAP helicopters patrolled the city and its surroundings.[43] At the airport, in the area reserved for domestic flights, all passengers were subjected to intense surveillance by the DGS.

According to the newspaper, Marcello called a meeting of the Council of Ministers for the afternoon of the 16th (Saturday) in São Bento to analyse the situation. A lengthy meeting started around 5 pm and only at 8 pm did the members of the government begin to leave the usual place of work of the President of the Council. The journalist noted the presence of the ministers of Overseas Territories, Defence, Navy, Interior, State, Education, and concluded that if the Minister of Foreign Affairs was in Brazil and the Minister of Corporations was in Venezuela, it could be seen that the entire government had interrupted their weekend. This fact alone showed the scale of the government's shock at the Caldas revolt, despite the fact that the President of the Council later minimised it in his memoirs and in the Council of Ministers meeting itself. For Caetano, the fact that only one military unit had revolted and that it was influenced by officers from outside the unit was positive, as was the fact that the remaining units had obeyed the government's orders and that there had been no public unrest.[44] But if we add to the ministers' meeting the fact that Caetano and Thomaz moved during the night to a safe place, we get the idea that the authorities were surprised and had no idea of the dimensions of the coup, which was also completely uncoordinated. However, Caetano did not fail to underline in his memoirs that the Caldas revolt could not be underestimated, as the officers that provoked it would certainly have other supporters that would not disarm, and the revolt was also a sign of the military's state of mind in which many officers were not willing to continue the war in the Overseas.[45]

Regarding Belém Palace, the newspaper continued, 'apparently everything was calm,' Admiral Américo Thomaz was presumably at his private residence in Restelo (Lisbon), where the usual security measures were considerably reinforced.

The government only issued a statement on the situation at 19:00 of the 17th, through a note from the Secretariat of State for Information and Tourism, which said the following: for 14 hours (from 02:00 am until around 04:00 pm) there was insubordination at RI5 in Caldas da Rainha. The government said that the regime of strict prevention had come into force from 05:00 (it may have started much earlier as previously described by other sources) with police reinforcement at the entrances north of Lisbon and that from 07:00 to 09:00 traffic was cut off on the northern motorway. Between 09:00 and 11:00 all cars were checked. Despite this, the front-page headline closed the issue: 'After the surrender of the officers who rebelled in Caldas da Rainha order reigns throughout the country.' According to the government, forces from that unit, under the command of majors and integrating officers belonging to other units in the country, had rebelled. The forces arrived near the start of the motorway in Vila Franca de Xira and knowing of a strong blockade at the exit for Lisbon near the airport, under the command of the Army Chief of Staff, General Paiva Brandão, retreated.

In the Caldas da Rainha barracks the power and water was cut off and an Air Force helicopter flew over the place, but the population 'remained unaware of the serious events that ended with the surrender of the junior officers.' There

Brigadier Pedro Serrano, of the Tomar Military Region, demands the surrender of the Caldas insurgents on 16 March. The photo was taken by an RI5 soldier who was inside the barracks. (RI5)

Another view of the siege of the Caldas barracks on 16 March. Despite some resistance, the Caldas-based military had no choice but to surrender. (RI5)

were no incidents or military or civilian casualties. In the middle of the afternoon of 16 March, the military rebels in Caldas surrendered to the forces of the Military Region of Tomar, who surrounded the barracks, and the adventure ended with the arrest of 180 men, including officers, sergeants, and soldiers.[46] Before the surrender, Casanova Ferreira gathered the officers who were in the barracks and told them that they were all going to be arrested and that they should say at the enquiry that they did what they did as a demonstration of displeasure for the dismissals of Spínola and Costa Gomes. And that is what they all said in the enquiry process in Trafaria prison.[47] This version is confirmed by Piedade Faria, one of the captains involved, who later confessed that the fuse that triggered the revolt was the dismissal by the regime of Costa Gomes and Spínola. The captain recalls that in several military units there was great anxiety about the measures that the government could take against the military and against the two generals in particular. When the two generals were dismissed, the reaction could only be revolt. He also said that Spínola was not aware of the revolt.[48] For Bordalo Xavier, one of the captains from Lamego, the big mistake on the night of 15 March was Ferreira da Silva's phone call to Lisbon saying that they were on wheels, which was not true. This phone call misled Manuel Monge and led the military linked to Spínola to take measures that proved disastrous. In Lamego, Bordalo Xavier reveals that they also had internal problems with the sabotage of vehicles by a mechanic sergeant who was a member of the Portuguese Legion. But the big problem was that they never received orders from the movement to carry out a forceful action.⁴⁹ Another of Lamego's captains, Monteiro Valente believed that the Caldas revolt was mainly motivated by officers linked to Spínola, such as Armando Marques Ramos, who created the environment for the revolt to take place. For this captain, Marques Ramos was one of the main instigators of the revolt and created a false image in Caldas that troops from Lamego were already on their way to Lisbon, which did not correspond to the truth.⁵⁰

Otelo recognised that the attempt ended with a highly negative balance for the MFA, but for him it had advantages, as he had the opportunity to see the government's reaction and the botched manner in which the forces mobilised by the Army Minister were positioned at the entrance to the capital. At that moment, Otelo became convinced that a well-planned and structured military action with a centralised command would quickly overcome any resistance that the regime managed to mobilise.⁵¹ Moreover, among the military personnel arrested only Manuel Monge belonged to the MFA Coordinating Committee. The authorities had managed to 'silence' the Caldas insurgents but had not annihilated the movement's leadership.

Arnaldo Costeira, who was in Viseu, also recognises that the Caldas revolt brought many lessons. Firstly, the inexistence of a clear chain of command had been a serious flaw. For Costeira it was unthinkable to mount a military revolt 'without a form of real and timely transmission of information and command instructions.'⁵² For the RI14 captain it was essential in future to take over a radio or television broadcasting station for the transmission of marching orders.

It is interesting to note that it was PIDE/DGS who detected the movement of the military column. That night, inspector Abílio Augusto Pires was still at the political police headquarters and was warned of the military movement by the Peniche post that reported the exit of a military column from Caldas da Rainha. From there, the inspector warned the ministers of Defence and of the Army and the general commander of GNR, who took the measures that are known.⁵³

In the aftermath of the events of 16 March, the Minister of National Defence sent a message to all commanders-in-chief in Angola, Guinea, Macau, Mozambique, Timor, Cape Verde, the Azores, and Madeira. Dated 17 March the letter stated that it was an addendum from the previous day – which is not in the dossier – in which he confirmed 'that complete order reigns and there have been no other manifestations of indiscipline.' Silva Cunha asked the commanders to inform him of the state of mind of the troops, and for special attention to contact between officers who tried to create a climate of unrest. He also said that there had been use of transmission centres of the Armed Forces. It ordered that if any commander had similar information, he should take 'immediate measures' to put an end to this procedure.⁵⁴ The answers the minister received were all along the lines of normality. The command of the Azores reported on 18 March that complete order reigned without any sign of foreseeing any alterations, the state of mind of the officers was one of loyalty to the command, and measures had been taken to verify security standards. In Madeira, there was nothing unusual. In the colonies, the commander of Guinea reported that there was no repercussion of the unrest in Caldas, and order and discipline reigned. If the 16 March event had not yet caused alarm, the issue of the book continued to be the subject of comment and there was an attitude of expectation with regard to developments in the mainland. The commander informed that the PAIGC had transmitted to all their commands orders to intensify the actions against the Portuguese troops in view of 'the great difficulties of the government and the Portuguese Armed Forces.' It also noted that no evidence of misuse of military transmissions had been detected. In Cape Verde, Angola, Macau, and Timor the situation was described only as normal or without abnormal facts.⁵⁵ In short, Marcello Caetano was convinced that it had all been an isolated act, but that it was a sign of the dissatisfaction present in the military forces.

Incredulity in the opposition, but some hope

In the Portuguese political opposition, namely the Portuguese Communist Party (*Partido Comunista Português*, PCP), the Caldas revolt was viewed with scepticism. The manifesto of the Executive Committee of the communists published in the second fortnight of March 1974 and reproduced in the April issue of the party's clandestine newspaper – *O Avante* – on the false start of the 'Caldas Column' constituted 'the final and public expression of the anti-military prejudice' that still persisted in the core of the PCP leadership on the eve of 25 April. In the manifesto one can read that 'the government and the regime will not fall by themselves, nor even less by the action of a few dozen army officers, even if brave and patriotic. The March 16 uprising shows this once again.'

From 1967, the PCP took measures to resume the party's work among the military. These measures made it possible to structure the connection with a small core of officers of the permanent staff and to organise those who were entering the Armed Forces, especially as militia officers, both in the metropolis and in the colonies. The party began to publish a printed leaflet entitled *Revolutionary Information for the Armed Forces* through which awareness and action against the war were developed and information was circulated on the resistance actions that were taking place in the barracks and also on the measures of the military commands. It was through this party structure that the PCP was able to follow very closely the captains' movement from the beginning and in its evolution.

According to Carlos Brito, responsible in the PCP's leadership for this structure, it allowed the PCP to exert some influence, but only in the restricted field of the elaboration of programmatic positions and no more than that. However, it kept the party in contact with military officers who occupied prominent positions in the captains' movement. The then communist leader stated that he knew 'the time when the leading structures of this movement woke up and started preparing the military uprising to overthrow the dictatorship.' But despite having informed the Executive Committee and the Secretariat, the Secretary-General, Álvaro Cunhal, so that adequate measures could be adopted for an appropriate positioning of the party, 'with great astonishment' the response that came from Paris (where Cunhal was in exile) was not only of great scepticism regarding the information but also full of recommendations to be on the alert for adventurist and putschist tendencies of the military that could harm the rise of the popular and democratic struggle. 'Cunhal's answers always came marked by a sententious scepticism,' Carlos Brito reported. This position 'almost on the eve of the 25th of April' meant that 'the central nucleus of the PCP leadership abroad did not recognise that the longed-for revolutionary or pre-revolutionary situation, always pointed to as an indispensable condition for the success of the revolution, had finally arrived.'

According to the then communist leader,

> … the Caldas attempt highlighted, more than the rashness of the military who left on time, was the weakness of the response given to it by the forces loyal to the regime. This was a new and great sign of weakness of the regime, which added to the almost

Álvaro Cunhal, leader of the Portuguese Communist Party, in a public appearance after the April revolution. Cunhal did not believe that the military could overthrow the regime and is why he devalued the Caldas revolt. (Revista do Povo collection)

Mário Soares, leader of the Portuguese socialist party and exiled in Germany, sensed that revolution could be on the way and that the regime could change in Portugal. After the revolution he quickly returned to the country and was one of the most popular politicians during the revolutionary period. (Revista do Povo collection)

impunity with which the military conspiracy was developed in several units.[56]

Brito also mentions that Cunhal was surprised, in Paris, by the military coup that overthrew the regime, since he underestimated the military factor in the overthrow of the dictatorship. There was even an intention on Cunhal's part to devalue the role of the military in comparison with the popular masses.[57] However, it is curious to see that after the revolution the PCP tried to influence certain leftist military sectors and was always very active in the military field trying to influence the military in favour of its positions.

From the point of view of the Americans in Lisbon and Washington, the Caldas revolt confirmed the 'invincibility' of the state's defensive system and the weakness of the opposition to the regime. Two days earlier, on 14 March, the director of the Office of Iberian Affairs, Ellwood Rabenold, had made a long statement about Portugal in the House of Representatives. He had previously analysed an embassy report on Spínola's book, admitted the political upheaval it had caused and mentioned the state of alert in the barracks. But he was adamant in his fundamental conclusion: 'I would like to make this observation: change in Portugal occurs very, very slowly, and I don't think it can be concluded that anything, even this book, will bring about change quickly.'[58]

And it was not only the Americans who were convinced that the regime was going to last. On the night of 24 April 1974, during a dinner in Bonn (Germany) with members of the social democratic party (SPD), the then German Minister of Finance told Mário Soares, founder, and leader of the Portuguese Socialist Party, that the Portuguese dictatorship was to last: 'The German government has information from our embassy in Lisbon, from our secret services, within NATO, and reliable information from the CIA and the British. All our informers assure us that the Portuguese dictatorship is set in stone and to last. Therefore, you exiles should have no illusions about it. It is dangerous for you to have any.' However, Mário Soares was convinced otherwise, but he could not convince his interlocutor that the end of the Portuguese regime was near.[59] But the proof that Soares was not discouraged about the possibility of the regime's fall is that after the release of Spínola's book, and already in the first days of March, he published in the French newspaper *Le Monde* an article entitled *Les masques tombent au Portugal* (*Masks fall in Portugal*) in which he wrote 'something is finally moving in Portugal.' A few days later, the Caldas rebels had a false start and Soares went to the news that night on France's second television channel (then all state-owned) to predict that his country might be on the verge of political change. Four days after 16 March, in a declaration to the international press he stated: 'The support base of Caetano's government has just shrunk again, and considerably, which makes us predict interesting developments of the Portuguese situation in the near future.'[60]

On the other hand, on another front there seemed to be some leaking of information. On 23 April 1974, the American diplomat Bob Bentley (who served in the Portuguese embassy between 1967 and 1971) passed through Lisbon and had lunch with an associate of Marcello Caetano who told him that the President of the Council had to resign in the next 24 to 48 hours because there was a military movement growing and the President of the Republic intended to form a new government. Bentley still tried to transmit this information to the embassy, but he was received by Richard Post, Deputy Chief of Mission, with whom he had bad relations, and the information ended up not reaching the embassy. However, he returned to Washington the following day and during his trip he wrote a letter to Secretary of State, Henry Kissinger, which he had delivered in his own hand, and which read 'there is going to be regime change in Portugal.'[61]

Calm in the Metropolis

Meanwhile, on 20 March, Marcello Caetano wrote to his Spanish friend Laureano López Rodó, professor at the University of Madrid and, at the time, ambassador to Vienna from Austria, and the tone is much less convinced as to the durability of the regime: 'I have lived through difficult days, but thanks to the support of the Portuguese people and the loyalty of the Armed Forces I have been winning. In the serious international situation that you know well, these internal discussions are criminal.'[62]

Also on 20 March, the security forces ceased their state of security of alert and moved to a state of vigilance, while the determinations on the care to be taken with the displacement of personnel were maintained.[63]

A sign that the government sensed that its end was near is mirrored in Foreign Minister Rui Patrício's venting a few days after 16 March to ambassador Villas-Boas. This diplomat was preparing to go to London to engage in secret talks with Guinea-Bissau's PAIGC in yet another contradiction of the regime. Villas-Boas said he would report back within a week. Rui Patrício replied: 'if I then still sit in this chair.'[64]

The situation in Portugal attracted the attention of foreign media and Bruce Loudon, who wrote for British newspapers, continued to be prolix in his coverage of events. On 17 March, he wrote in *The Sunday Telegraph* that Costa Gomes and Spínola were the two immediate victims of the crisis in the Portuguese Armed Forces, but that the events of the last few weeks could have wider implications. The journalist was again talking about an internal conflict within the regime itself between two factions: a conservative one that had ruled the country for the last 50 years and a liberal one that wanted change. With the dismissal of Costa Gomes and Spínola, the conservatives, led by Américo Thomaz, had emerged as winners and Caetano, considered to be a moderate, was another victim. The head of the executive had tried to find a graceful way out of the crisis by promoting the ceremony of military loyalty to the government, but with Costa Gomes and Spínola refusing to attend, he had no choice but to dismiss the two generals. Loudon considered that Thomaz was the brake to any further liberalisation of the regime and that this could cause problems to Caetano who wanted to reform the country. For the British journalist, there was no doubt that Américo Thomaz had emerged much stronger from this crisis, which could be seen in the appointment of General Luz Cunha as CEMGFA, a man close to Thomaz, associated with conservative sectors and who only a few months ago had his name implicated in a plot against Caetano. It was therefore expected that Américo Thomaz would now keep a closer eye on the head of the executive, blocking any reform that did not please the conservative sector. Loudon also pointed out that Spínola's book had become a political best-seller and that, however much the government tried to mitigate its effects, it would have to learn to live with the book. As for Spínola, he hoped that the book would provoke intelligent discussions about the future. In a conversation he had with the journalist a few days earlier, the general stressed that the book was not a political testament and that he hoped it would become a basis for thinking about the future of the Overseas Territories. Spínola believed that if the government did not have the capacity to change and adapt to circumstances, it ran the serious risk of losing the overseas domains, as had happened in India in 1961. Loudon ended the article by stating that Spínola's radical ideas had support at all levels of the Armed Forces, especially among the combatants who had been in Africa on the war fronts. They were the ones who believed that Spínola's proposals, in the absence of others, were a good starting point for discussion. But the most worrying signs of some kind of instability in Portugal were in the impact that the book had caused in the country, with fears that Spínola's next move could be a coup d'état.[65] It is clear from the text, that Loudon wrote the article a few hours before the revolt in Caldas on 16 March, but it was clear that the journalist had captured the conspiratorial atmosphere that reigned in the Portuguese capital at that time.

The article went down badly with the Secretary of State for Information and Tourism. We know this from a letter that Bruce Loudon himself wrote to the director of the Information and Tourism Services, Pedro Feytor Pinto, on 27 March. In this letter, the journalist complains about 'voices' that, within the Secretariat of State, had organised themselves against the article, and expresses his displeasure that these 'voices' had not said anything in the past, when Loudon had done work defending the Portuguese Overseas Territories and the permanence of Portugal in these territories. In the letter, the journalist also expressed his wish to talk to Feytor Pinto about these issues and asked him to talk to Marcello Caetano, so that the President of the Council could grant him an off-the-record interview, the request for which had been made in February.[66] Feytor Pinto sent a copy of the missive to Marcello Caetano with a personal comment in which he considered that there was nothing 'against the man,' although he said that he read an article which would have been much better if he had not written it. He also said that Loudon was with Jorge Jardim 'when quite compromising things were found,' but that this reason alone was not enough to take measures against the journalist. Feytor Pinto also recalled that the Ministry of Foreign Affairs and the Secretariat of State itself consider that Loudon 'has rendered very relevant services to the Portuguese cause' and that 'under these circumstances, and if he receives no instructions to the contrary,' he intended to receive the journalist 'telling him that there is nothing against him but rumours to which he should not listen.'[67]

However, Bruce Loudon was not the only journalist following the situation in Lisbon and Harold Sieve also wrote in the same edition of *The Sunday Telegraph,* on 17 March, that the Caldas coup had

Bruce Loudon, journalist and correspondent for *The Daily Telegraph* in Lisbon. (Telegraph Library)

failed. The journalist described a confrontation between troops from the Caldas Regiment of Infantry 5 and Cavalry 7 from the capital, in the vicinity of Lisbon airport, but that it had been a non-violent clash. Harold Sieve says that Spínola was not involved in the revolt as he had spent the night at home. The British journalist believed that the military uprising was provoked by the removal of Costa Gomes and Spínola, which led to protests in various barracks and a revolt in the Caldas regiment. However, the operation had failed due to lack of planning and coordination. The journalist makes several factual errors in the news, but ends the text saying that, despite the fiasco, the serious political-military crisis in Portugal was far from over and that the future evolution of the situation would depend on the behaviour of General Spínola.[68]

Two days later, on 19 March, the journalist reported in *The Daily Telegraph* on the purge in the Armed Forces with the arrest of 30 officers and 200 men who were supposedly involved in the Caldas revolt. According to the journalist, Spínola had advised his 'young Turks' to avoid protests but had not publicly dissociated himself from the rebel officers who had carried out the revolt in his name, which was significant. Had he taken this attitude, he would have comforted Marcello Caetano, who was now in the hands of the right-wing of the regime that opposed a political solution to the conflicts in Africa.[69]

We can see that the following day Harold Sieve also wrote in the same newspaper about the extent of the purge and points out that the dissenters in the Army were far from being limited to the Caldas regiment that had revolted. Dissatisfaction was also affecting other units, with the government having transferred officers to distant garrisons in the north of the country, in the Azores and even to Guinea. According to a reliable source, an entire platoon (in fact it had been a company) had recently refused to embark for Guinea, being forced to board the plane at gunpoint, a sign that the regime might have to face more problems of indiscipline in the military forces.[70]

The Portuguese government was also trying to reassure the diplomatic corps accredited in the country, and on 21 March it called in the military attaché of the French embassy. The summons came from the Under-Secretary of State for the Army, Viana de Lemos, who wanted to 'clarify biased information published in the press' about the scale of the events that had upset the army. The French officer passed the information on to the ambassador Bernard Durand, who wrote a telegram to Paris in which he reported that although order had apparently been restored in the army, a certain tension persisted.[71]

Eight days after this communication, the ambassador sent a letter to the French Minister of Foreign Affairs about the politicisation of the captains' movement after having received a manifesto dated 11 March, distributed clandestinely by the captains' movement, and which reached the embassy on 22 March. The document revealed the depth of resentment, without it being possible yet to see how representative it was of its authors. It stressed the apolitical character of the military institution, openly accused the government of humiliating the Army by making it bear the responsibility for the current difficulties in Overseas and of isolating the nation. The document also said that the power does not have the means for the measure of its policy and victory was impossible by arms. Inspired by Spínola's arguments, it also stated that the solution to the overseas problem was political and defended the right of the people to govern themselves. It also defended an urgent reform of the country's institutions towards democratisation.[72]

At the Ministry of the Interior, in Lisbon, minister Moreira Baptista was receiving several requests for more vigilance from the PSP (on 21 March) and on the following day a letter, dated 16 March, also from the PSP, regarding the report of the events at the RI5 in Caldas da Rainha, and on 25 March another letter, dated 19 March, with reports on military events in Lamego recorded on 16 March. On the 26th, he received the union activities registered in the workers' environment of Marinha Grande. On 28 March, he received a letter from Amnesty International about the detention of Nuno Teotónio Pereira, a leading figure in the democratic opposition to the regime.[73]

Regarding the outgoing correspondence, on 19 March Moreira Baptista sent an official letter to the director of the DGS, to whom he sent the PERINTREP – periodic intelligence report – regarding the period between 9 and 16 March, carried out by the General Command of the PSP. He also sent a photocopy of a PSP information report on possible clandestine meetings in a house in a vineyard in Bárrio – Alcobaça, to the Chief of Staff of the Minister of the Army. He also sent the DGS the 'PERINTREP' of the General Command of the PSP, from 2–9 March.[74] Consulting the registry books of the correspondence received and sent by the minister during this period, one can see that routine continues to mark the days.

Mission to London

On another front, on 24 March, ambassador José Manuel Villas-Boas left for London on a secret mission. He had been summoned to Lisbon (he was in a meeting in Geneva) by the Minister of Foreign Affairs, Rui Patrício, to deal with a highly secret matter 'that in Portugal was only known to three people: Marcello Caetano, himself (the minister) and the Director-General of Political Affairs,' Ambassador João de Freitas Cruz.[75] Villas-Boas's mission was to go to London to speak with representatives of the PAIGC guerrillas in exile to negotiate a possible independence for the Portuguese colony. The initiative for this meeting had come from diplomats from the British embassy in Lisbon, who had visited Guinea in February 1974 to learn about the military situation on the ground. During this visit, the British diplomats proved to be well informed about the regime's problems, commenting that Portugal was currently fighting three wars: that of the captains, that of the generals and that of Africa. Regarding the possibility of negotiations with the PAIGC, the Portuguese replied that 'our dialogue is with the people of Guinea, and not with those who have serious commitments to foreign powers.'[76] The reply did not convince the British, given that shortly after the visit, the British ambassador in Lisbon contacted Rui Patrício to propose a meeting in London between the PAIGC and a representative of the Portuguese government.[77] Patrício then consulted Marcello Caetano about this meeting and the President of the Council authorised a Portuguese emissary to go to the British capital. Patrício explained to Villas-Boas that Portugal was losing the war in Guinea, faced with a guerrilla group heavily armed with surface-to-air missiles, and that it was necessary to begin talks with the PAIGC, which were to be kept in the utmost secrecy. Patrício later confessed that a very difficult political and military situation required all kinds of initiatives and that he took advantage of British goodwill to make contacts with the PAIGC, informing the head of government beforehand, who did not reject the idea.[78] It was in this context that Villas-Boas was chosen as the minister's special emissary to travel to London to speak with the Guineans, bringing with him an offer of independence for Guinea-Bissau in exchange for a ceasefire, but without mentioning specific dates.[79]

Dolphin Square flats and gardens in London. It was in this area of the British capital that the Portuguese envoy met with the PAIGC delegation. (José Matos collection)

Rui Patrício was responsible for sending Villas-Boas to London to meet with a PAIGC delegation. The meeting was agreed by Marcello Caetano, although the Portuguese ruler had little interest in negotiating with the PAIGC. (José Matos collection)

Villas-Boas arrived in London on 24 March and was accompanied by a British secret service (MI6) agent. Two days later he was taken to a flat, in London's Dolphin Square, an area of brown flats, known as a place for romantic encounters. It was a discreet place, ideal for a secret meeting. It was here that Villas-Boas met with the Guinean delegation composed of Vítor Saúde Maria, Foreign Minister of the PAIGC, Silvino Manuel da Luz and Gil Fernandes.

The first difficulty he encountered was that the Guineans were expecting the Portuguese minister Rui Patrício, which is why they sent Vítor Saúde, but Villas-Boas pointed out that he was representing the minister and was speaking on his behalf, but the Guineans wanted negotiations at the highest level that would lead Portugal to recognise the PAIGC government in exile.[80]

Thus, this first meeting took place in a tense atmosphere and a new meeting was scheduled for the following day, where Vítor Saúde was no longer present, thus responding to the absence of Rui Patrício. Obviously, the Guinean delegation was only interested in full independence and the 'immediate establishment of a calendar leading to it. Only this could lead them to accept a ceasefire,' said Villas-Boas. Even so, the Portuguese representative managed to set a new meeting for early May in the British capital to continue the talks.[81] Aristides Pereira, who led the PAIGC, at the time after the death of Amilcar Cabral, later admitted that these contacts could never produce great results because the Portuguese wanted to separate the issue of the independence of Guinea from that of Cape Verde, while the party was fighting for the independence of the two territories.[82]

For Calvet Magalhães, who was Secretary-General of the Ministry of Foreign Affairs at the time and who was also involved in the preparation of the mission to London, 'the meaning and scope' of the talks in the British capital should be assessed in the context in which the Portuguese government was hoping to receive the Redeye missiles to use in Guinea. Officially, the negotiations with the US for the supply of this type of military material had failed, but Portugal hoped to receive them covertly, which in his opinion would change the military situation in Guinea once again, providing protection for Portuguese troops in case of air attack.[83] Calvet said that Villas-Boas was unaware of this fact and that 'it is going too far to say that Marcello Caetano had decided to negotiate the independence of Guinea'.[84] It thus seems that the regime only wanted to gain time to receive the missiles and continue the war with them. As we have seen previously, the range of acquisitions planned at this time was large and included several types of war material, using the financing of the South African loan, material that would reinforce the Portuguese troops in Guinea and the other colonies.

On 28 March João de Freitas Cruz, Director General of Political Affairs, left a written note about a conversation with the counsellor of the US embassy in Lisbon. Freitas Cruz said that nothing that happened domestically affected the Portuguese position on the issue of negotiating the Azores.[85] He noted, however, that the interlocutor alluded to the problems raised by the publication of Spínola's book and mentioned that he had cancelled the dinner with the two generals, scheduled for 18 March. He stressed that he was speaking in a personal capacity and said that if Portugal took 'an extreme right-wing government line' the country could not count on the slightest support from the United States, and that in the negotiations for the renewal of the Azores agreement the Americans would have to be very careful not to appear to be giving the Portuguese a 'pat on the back'. Freitas Cruz replied that his fears 'of such a far-right government line seemed unfounded.'[86]

The fear of a right-wing coup in Portugal had already been reported a few months earlier by the chargé d'affaires of the American embassy in Lisbon, Richard Post. In late 1973, Post informed his

Carlos Fabião, was one of the main figures of the MFA and responsible in December 1973 for denouncing a coup that was being prepared by conservative sectors of the regime. After the revolution he held the post of Chief of Staff of the Army. (AEI)

superiors of a coup attempt led by military and political figures linked to the right-wing of the regime, who were dissatisfied with Marcello Caetano's policy in Africa. These figures would have pressured the President of the Republic to replace Caetano with Adriano Moreira, who had been Minister of Overseas under Salazar, or with General Kaúlza de Arriaga, until recently commander-in-chief of the Armed Forces in Mozambique. Post also identified other personalities involved such as generals Silvino Silvério Marques and Luz Cunha and the former Minister of Foreign Affairs, Franco Nogueira. Kaúlza de Arriaga had tried to convince Spínola to join the coup, but the latter refused, as he had another vision for Africa. The plan had been publicly denounced on 17 December 1973, by Major Carlos Fabião (a denunciation made at the Institute for Advanced Military Studies during a class, in which Fabião publicly denounced that a military coup was being prepared, led by Kaúlza de Arriaga, and supported by Silvino Silvério Marques, Luz Cunha and Henrique Troni, with the aim of eliminating Costa Gomes and António de Spínola). Despite everything, Post ended the information stating that it was highly probable that Caetano would emerge from this crisis strengthened in his political position.[87]

Meanwhile, in mid-January 1974, the new American ambassador, Stuart Nash Scott, a 68-year-old New York lawyer and friend of Richard Nixon, arrived in the Portuguese capital. On 5 February he had his first conversation with Marcello Caetano, who noted that Scott had arrived in Portugal at a time when relations between Lisbon and Washington were very good, but also at a delicate moment in the negotiations for the renewal of the Azores Agreement that were underway (as seen earlier). Caetano complained that the 1971 agreement was not good for Portugal. Scott agreed that relations between the two countries were going through a very good phase and that the negotiations around the Azores base were delicate, but that he hoped that the US government could respond to Portuguese wishes. Caetano also complained that the US Congress was terrible at passing legislation hostile to Portugal, but Scott replied that the White House had always come out against such legislation.[88] However, what worried the Portuguese regime at the time was Washington's position of not supplying any type of weapons to Portugal, which left the Portuguese rulers exasperated. Scott sensed this in a conversation he had with Rui Patrício on 4 March, in which the Portuguese minister argued that the American embargo made no sense, given that Portugal had been threatened in Guinea and Angola by foreign countries (Guinea-Conakry and Zaire) and that it needed weapons to defend itself, namely against air attacks and armoured vehicles. He also complained that the 1971 Azores Agreement had been bad for Portugal and that because of this, there was a feeling in public opinion against renewing the agreement, which also extended to the military. Patrício was not sorry that he had supported the airlift to Israel during the war against the Arab countries in 1973 and would do the same again if he had to, but this support had disastrous consequences for Portugal, not only because of the oil embargo, but also because the communist countries had stepped up their aid to the insurgent movements fighting Portuguese troops in Africa. So, Portugal needed weapons and Patrício felt that the US had to help. Scott quickly realised that the Portuguese minister was playing all or nothing to modify the embargo.[89] Despite Patrício's appeals, the embargo remained in place, creating difficulties for the Portuguese regime in acquiring arms. The State Department was not very receptive to any supply and Kissinger even sent a message to the American embassy in Lisbon confirming the arms embargo and the impossibility of supplying the Redeye missiles that Portugal wanted so badly,[90] although Kissinger later found a way to supply them secretly.

In Lisbon, the American ambassador continued to monitor the evolution of the political situation in Portugal and did not fail to report to the State Department the impacts of the publication of the book that Spínola had written and the Caldas revolt. Scott acknowledged that there was a serious political crisis in Portugal motivated by Spínola's book and the 16 March revolt and that this could affect the renegotiation of the Azores Agreement. On 19 March, the American diplomat drew attention to the political crisis in the country with the right-wing of the regime pressuring Américo Thomaz to dismiss Caetano, although this dismissal could provoke a military reaction from sectors linked to Spínola and Costa Gomes. The ambassador considered that the right-wing of the regime had little understanding of the American position and the problems in Congress, and that they were convinced that Portugal was fighting in Africa against communism, in favour of NATO and the United States. Thus, if this group took power, it would not hesitate to demand greater support from the Americans in exchange for the Lajes base, which if not granted could lead to the end of the agreement with the USA. Scott therefore considered that a swing of the regime to the right would be harmful to American interests and would leave Portugal even more isolated in the international context.[91]

On 30 March, the ambassador sent a new telegram to Washington, in which he analysed the political and economic situation in Portugal and pointed out that the publication of Spínola's book and subsequent events caused a shake-up in Portuguese political life and its 'apparent unchanging stability.' Scott considered that the right-wing of the regime was on the rise after the resignation of Spínola and Costa Gomes and that Caetano's room for manoeuvre had been substantially reduced. It was true that Marcello Caetano's government still had some chance of survival, although it was very much limited by the pressures from the most conservative sectors of the regime. However, in Scott's analysis, the possibility of a new military revolt 'better planned and less impulsive' than the Caldas revolt was not completely ruled out, but he did not forget that the leadership of the movement 'had, for the moment, been decapitated

During the Caldas revolt, Otelo was not detected by the political police, leaving him free to plan the next coup, which would be fatal for the regime. (Revista do Povo collection)

Ernesto de Melo Antunes with Netherlands Minister of Foreign Affairs, Max van der Stoel, in May 1975. Melo Antunes was the main ideologist of the MFA and responsible for the first political programme. By order of the regime, he was sent to the Azores Islands, returning to the mainland after the military coup. In the post-revolutionary period, he would be the Minister of Foreign Affairs. (Nationaal Archief)

in the metropolis.' The diplomat acknowledged for the first time the existence of the 'officers' movement' and there were indications that the movement was gaining support among the military in the Overseas Territories, after the arrests on 16 March, some carried out by PIDE/DGS, which had caused unease in military circles. As for the possibility of a coup from the more conservative sector of the regime, or of a greater domination by this group in the governance of the country, this seemed difficult, since it could provoke a military reaction from the opposing side. Regarding the President of the Council, Scott hoped that Caetano would gradually emerge from his weakened position and adopt a more liberal policy towards Africa in the long term (whether he wanted to or not), prompted by the dynamics of change that Spínola's book had brought about in Portuguese society.[92] The ambassador's analysis showed, however, that the Americans did not have a profound knowledge of what was happening within the Armed Forces, where the movement of captains already presented an unstoppable dynamic towards regime change. Contrary to what Scott thought, Marcello Caetano's government was only weeks away from falling.

After the attempted coup in Caldas, many of the Spinolist officers involved were imprisoned in the Trafaria fort. The political power focused its attention on them since it was certain that Spínola controlled the movement. This attitude benefited the movement because it diverted attention from other MFA military officers who were conspiring against the government. Otelo was one of those who escaped and was thus free to plan the next coup.

In the opinion of Manuel Maria Múrias, an admirer of Salazar, the failure of 16 March would be the 'extraordinary' opportunity that the government had to disarticulate the MFA. Múrias said that:

> ... any reasonably well-informed person knew what was going on: a secret shared by two hundred people is not a secret – it is a luminous announcement. So, it is very strange that in the face of events, the President of the Republic, the President of the Council, and the government failed to act. The main conspiracy went unpunished. At dawn on April 25, the revolution was in the streets, without any visible resistance.[93]

For the French embassy in Portugal, the country was going through an undeniable crisis. On 18 March, a telegram was sent with the title 'the Portuguese crisis,' which stated that the shake-up the regime had suffered last week (16 March) with the explosion of discontent in military circles contrasted with the calm of an apathetic population. The ambassador ended by saying that Portuguese political life was at a turning point.[94]

Otelo revealed that, in the case of the enquiry processes regarding the graduates that had been taken to the military camp of Santa Margarida, these were initiated quickly and, after two weeks, the military that had been detained were finally released and placed in other units. In the MFA leader's analysis, these and other transfers benefited 'the advance of the military mass agitation' of the movement's officers.

On 18 March, Otelo Saraiva de Carvalho and Vítor Alves circulated circular no. 2/74, which they had written the day before, summarising the most important events in the history of the movement, such as the transfer of the four officers, an 'arbitrariness' that the MFA tried to refuse and that provoked reactions at the level of the authorities, revealing 'their intolerance, their total lack of understanding of the problems.' Later, on 14 March, the military had witnessed, 'indignantly,' a demonstration by generals who claimed to represent the Armed Forces and who 'represented nothing but themselves and their lack of civic and moral courage.' The circular argued that the 'unqualified' demonstration had been 'the immediate cause of the most recent events, which led some generous and selfless but excessively impatient comrades to try to resolve the situation immediately.' However, he continued, the action 'was not useless.' It served to clearly define the fields in presence, to reveal 'the contradictions in which the Army is struggling, and – as it is 'the mirror of the Nation' – the general crisis of the country. The document also criticised the meddling of the political police, which it considered having been triggered by the Minister and Under-Secretary of State for the Army and which made arrests without a legal warrant, called in the GNR, which it sent against RI5, and which surrounded the Military Academy and the Portuguese Legion and also collaborated in following the forces of RI5 returning to Caldas da Rainha. 'The action they unleashed was not useless' and despite the repression (200 arrested) it would not be possible to stop what was 'already irreversible.' Addressing the three branches of the Portuguese forces, the MFA leadership stated that the events allowed the movement to proceed 'with more security and realism.' It appealed for cohesion and firmness in relation to the objectives.[95] The circular written by Vítor Alves and Otelo to the remaining

Major Vítor Alves at the time he was Minister of Education and Scientific Research, after the April revolution. Vítor Alves was an important member of the MFA and was responsible for the political programme of the movement after the departure of Melo Antunes to the Azores Islands. (Flama archive)

Marcello Caetano doing the 'family talk' on Portuguese television. (Bild archive)

elements of the movement was silent on the drafting of a political programme, but on the night of 18 March Vítor Alves and Otelo met Melo Antunes and asked him to draw up a political programme. Melo Antunes was apprehensive, as he thought that, after 16 March, the political police would pursue and investigate other elements of the MFA, with the serious risk of the movement falling apart, but Otelo tried to encourage him by telling him that the Caldas coup had been a great lesson and that the movement had the conditions to move forward.[96]

On the night of 22 March, Melo Antunes read the first version of the MFA political programme at a meeting at Vítor Alves's house with a small group of Army, Navy, and Air Force officers. Those present approved the programme and Melo Antunes left that same night for the Azores, by decision of the Army General Staff. A punishment he was suffering because he was also an officer suspected of links to the movement.

As for the programme, as we shall see, it would remain in the hands of Vítor Alves to be refined and perfected with contributions from various sources until it reached the final version, which would be typed by Major Hugo Santos, the document being ready for final adjustments on 21 April.[97]

Two days after the meeting at Vítor Alves's house, Otelo confessed, in a new meeting, that no one had any doubts about the need for an armed revolution. At this meeting, it was decided that Otelo would be responsible for drawing up the operational plan and the order of operations, and Vítor Alves would be in charge of the political programme, and that the coup would take place between 20 and 29 April. During the meeting, the military also discussed the fact that they had neglected to prepare a situation study and decided that they would end the information transmitted by circular. The attitude to take would be to pass on the idea that the movement had disarticulated, after the arrest of its leaders, so that the Government would think it had neutralised the movement. According to Otelo, everyone agreed to reach 'the last consequences, to take up arms, to carry out a coup d'état.'[98]

The Last Family Conversation

On 28 March, Marcello Caetano uttered his last 'family talk' on Portuguese radio and television, in a premonitory tone and as a balance of his mandate. He returned to his theses on the defence of Overseas Territories, which he had mentioned in his speech to the National Assembly on 5 March, and justified the course taken during his mandate: 'Looking at the work carried out in the five and a half years of government (...) I am left with the peace of mind of having always sought to uprightly fulfil my duty towards the country, which is the same as saying towards the Portuguese people.' Marcello continued his assessment and alluded to the 'profound transformation of national life in all sectors' although he pointed out that change came at the cost of a change in mentalities, which for the President of the Council did not mean progress. He pointed out, before going on to make an incursion into overseas policy:

> The improvement in the economic and social conditions of Portuguese life has been processed in a climate of difficulties of all kinds – external and internal – in a world in the grip of a generalized and uncontrollable rise in prices, which corresponds to the crisis in the value of currencies, in a politically agitated time in which Portugal is forced to sustain the defence of a large part of the national territory.

Marcello said that the nation had 'refused' to abandon overseas lands, particularly Angola and Mozambique, 'two great provinces' where thousands of families had settled and which the country must defend. In this part of his speech, Marcello criticised the international press and adversaries who, 'regarding the publication in Portugal of a book [*Portugal and the Future*, by Spínola] in which an analysis is made of our position regarding the overseas problem' rushed to 'everything that in that analysis appeared to be favourable to their theses.' On the one hand, he said, there was nothing else to be done but the pure and simple abandonment of Overseas Territories, and on the other, they rejected any solution other than the immediate handing over of Overseas Territories to the so-called 'liberation' movements. Foreseeing the end, he pointed out:

> What all the foreigners, desirous of seeing us stripped of Overseas Territories, are playing at is the collapse of the rearguard in Portugal. This was seen in the enthusiasm with which the media from so many countries followed and increased the military episode that the thoughtlessness and perhaps the naivety of some officers unfortunately produced a few days ago in Caldas.

He also took the opportunity to launch 'an attack' on the defenders of freedom of expression, alleging that at stake was 'the safety of our people' who are fighting the war against 'terrorists.' And he returned

In 1974, Bernard Durand was the French ambassador in Lisbon and constantly informed Paris about the situation in Portugal. (Keystone Press Agency)

to the uprising in Caldas, an ill-considered act for 'not considering that in times of subversive war any manifestation of indiscipline assumes particular gravity. It was thoughtless, because they did not consider that there are political schemers, inside and outside, ready to exploit every episode to their advantage, to create internal dissensions and undermine the foundations of the State, and to benefit foreign interests.' After once again reviewing the memories of his trip to the colonies in 1969, Marcello ended his speech by saying that 'for as long as he holds this post' he would always bear in mind the 'Portuguese overseas, in mind and in heart.'[99]

The following day some reactions to the 'family talk' would arrive at his office. The president of the Supreme Administrative Court, Judge Álvaro Rodrigues Tavares, sent him a postcard of admiration for his speech the previous evening:

At this time of crisis and when Portugal is facing crucial vicissitudes, it could not be without deep emotion that Maria da Luz [his wife] and I heard you yesterday define the gravity of the situation and the President's position in the face of it. As friends and Portuguese, we accompany you in these moments when responsibilities assume special equity and at the same time demand the utmost courage and serenity. We well know, and from direct experience, that the higher they are, the more isolated you are when taking the respective decisions.[100]

In another letter dated 29 March, from Alfragide, the sender, journalist Eduardo Metzner Leone, said that he 'waited for the family conversation' to make a criticism: 'We are witnessing an active and aggressive improvement of the opposition press, which the situationist information has not been able to confront. Thus, in the competition that has been established, the government and its programme lose every day.' He ended his letter by stating that he had 'well-founded fears that everything is going to go from bad to worse.' He reiterated to the President of the Council that he would be at the government's full disposal as long as it continued with all possible means to defend Overseas Territories.[101]

On 5 April, the French ambassador in Lisbon, Bernard Durand, told his foreign minister about all the events in Portuguese political life and pointed out that Marcello's televised address had not responded to the concerns of the Portuguese, who were expecting an answer to questions following the events of the last month. The diplomat said that the head of the executive dealt only briefly with the subject, devoting much of his speech to an apologia for his management and made moral and philosophical considerations, invoked the titanic efforts to ensure economic development and defended, once again, the maintenance of the overseas territories within the national community.

Caetano also said that Spínola's book, which was widely publicised in the international press, did not give credence to the federal solution that the book advocated. The ambassador also noted that the President of the Council defended that the information with restrictions was justified by the fact that the country was at war. Marcello also referred to division in the Armed Forces and said that the attitude taken by the military in Caldas was a thoughtless move in time of war or underground manoeuvres by foreign powers. For the French diplomat, the leader had not changed his position, and everything seemed to be happening as if he ignored the lesson of the military and the undeniable weakening of his government.[102]

In fact, Marcello Caetano continued as if nothing had happened. On 31 March, he would appear in public, at the Alvalade Stadium, in Lisbon, to watch the football match between Sporting and Benfica, where he received a great ovation from the public present.[103] Marcello was obviously delighted with the reception he received at the stadium and must have thought that the people were with him. But while the President of the Council was encouraged by the applause of the crowd, Otelo began writing the order of operations for 25 April.

3
BETWEEN TANKS AND FLOWERS

After the failure of Caldas da Rainha, Otelo realised that there was no time to lose. During the intense month of April, the strategist of the revolution spent a great deal of time in contact with the government forces to reconnoitre and gather information about its military organisation. Thus, he received the 'operational picture of the PSP's organic structure,' the pictures of the 'Army's intervention force' and the 'government's reserve force' existing throughout the country, 'the layout of the Portuguese Legion forces on the continent and the latest movements of war material, namely the picture of the distribution of radio transmission material by the Army's military units.' This information was taken from the Army General Staff by MFA officers who worked in that organ. In this way, Otelo obtained privileged information to prepare the order of operations. He also tried to obtain information about the GNR, using a cousin – Major Velasco – who was stationed at the GNR headquarters in Carmo, Lisbon. Velasco ended up providing his cousin with a series of precious pieces of information that allowed Otelo to have in-depth knowledge of the GNR units and sub-units, their personnel, weaponry, timetables, periods of shift and what type of missions they would perform in the event of a coup attempt. He also discovered that of the 38 Shorland Mk 3 armoured patrol cars

A US-made M47 Patton tank fitted with a 90 mm gun. In 1974 it was the main battle tank of the Portuguese Army and was engaged in the April revolution by troops loyal to the regime. This M47 belongs to the Cavalry Practical School of Santarém but was not involved in the 25 April revolution. (Miranda Castela collection/Archive of the Assembly of the Republic)

The main Portuguese armoured vehicles of the era seen participating in an exercise. In the foreground, an AML Panhard, followed by an EBR Panhard and at the end an EBR-ETT, an armoured personnel carrier built on the same chassis as the EBR armoured car. (NATO collection)

ordered in England to equip the GNR, few were already assembled and operational in Lisbon.[1]

Otelo was also concerned to find out which units in the capital were in favour of the movement and which were against it. He was informed that he could only count on the 2nd Regiment of Lancers (Military Police) if its commanders were neutralised. This regiment was commanded by Colonel Pinto Bessa, a man loyal to the regime, but the regiment's officers also included Major Manuel Cruz Azevedo, who was the brother-in-law of the Under-Secretary of State for the Army, Viana de Lemos, and who would certainly not have sided with the MFA.[2] Another problematic unit was Cavalry Regiment 7 (RC7), where another of Viana de Lemos' brothers-in-law, Colonel António Romeiras Júnior, was based. This was the most dangerous unit for the movement, as it had received four operational M47 Patton tanks from Santa Margarida after the events in Caldas da Rainha. It also had in its inventory nine Panhard AML light armoured cars, three Panhard EBR armoured cars and four Chaimite V-200 armoured personnel carriers. The regiment had a one-hour readiness level and was commanded by officers loyal to the government.[3]

It should be noted that the M47 was the main battle tank of the Portuguese Army and were equipped with a 90mm cannon with

On 9 April 1974, the Revolutionary Brigades carried out an attack on the ship *Niassa* to delay the sending of troops to Guinea. (Flama archive)

a range of 1,200 metres, with no equivalent in firepower in the Portuguese cavalry units.[4] Practically only the Santa Margarida Brigade and the Santarém Cavalry forces had M47 tanks at their disposal. As we have seen, besides this armoured force, Cavalry Regiment 7 also had a group of Panhard AMLs, which were 4×4 armoured reconnaissance vehicles armed with two 7.62mm machine guns and a 60mm breech-loading gun-mortar.[5] The Panhard EBR, was an 8×8 armoured vehicle equipped with a 75mm cannon that had a range of 1,500 metres.[6] The Chaimite V-200 was a 4×4 armoured troop transport vehicle made in Portugal based on the American Cadillac Gage V-100.[7]

While the movement frantically prepared the coup, the government kept to its routine, not understanding what was going on. The Directorate General of Security itself, the famous PIDE/DGS, also failed to inform the government of the true gravity of the situation. The police forces also reported nothing special about the movement of the captains. The weekly information PERINTREP of the General Command of the PSP regarding the week between 6th and 13 April, was sent by Duarte Guedes Vaz – the chief of the cabinet of the Minister of the Interior – to the PIDE/DGS, where it arrived on 24 April, on the eve of the revolution, reported the existence of subversive leaflets in several cities of the country alluding to 1 May and other subjects, but nothing about movements in the military forces. In fact, in the paragraph referring to the adversary's possibilities it only said only 'not foreseen'. During that week, the PSP also said it seized from bookshops, stationers, tobacconists, newsagents, etc., 63 books and 94 subversive pamphlets, which were forbidden to circulate in the country and were picked up by the police.[8] The report was full of similar facts and references to subversive or suspicious activities detected, but nothing about a possible military revolt.

Also, without apparent suspicion of the military movement, the French embassy in Lisbon reported on 11 April 1974, in a letter to the Minister of Foreign Affairs, that there had been a wave of arrests in the Portuguese capital, citing information it had gathered that had not been reported in the press. The police arrested 40 people who were taking part in a meeting in a suburb of the capital.[9] Among the participants was Vítor Dias, who stood as a candidate in the last parliamentary elections on an opposition list and who in future would be a member and official of the Portuguese Communist Party.

On 19 April the embassy sent a new letter saying that the previous day there had been a new wave of arrests, this time of journalists working for the *República* newspaper, *Diário de Lisboa* and the *Seara Nova* magazine. Among the journalists arrested was Albano Lima.[10] He also told of the act of sabotage of the *Niassa*, the ship that was preparing to transport troops to Guinea, on 9 April. The act, which he referred to as an attack, caused some damage and delayed its departure for Guinea.[11]

The situation in Portugal was closely monitored in the French Ministry of Foreign Affairs as shown in an internal note from the Southern Europe sub-directorate dated 20 April. The note started by pointing out that the publication of Spínola's book provoked an uproar in the Army and the beginning of a mutiny, but that the authorities seemed to have the situation under control. In his last televised address, Caetano only briefly touched on the events of March (the Caldas revolt) and applauded the policy followed by the government. However, the events in question deserve more attention since they were directly related to the problem that dominated the internal and international life of the country: the overseas territories.

The note then talked about Spínola's career and the ideas of the book – which denounced the impossibility of achieving a victory in the Overseas War – to underline that the work revealed the seriousness of the malaise existing in part of the Army, especially in the middle officer ranks, who demanded above all the resolution of career and corporate problems. More or less clandestine meetings of the captains, coordinated by a 'Commission,' had taken place and a manifesto published by the captains' movement on 11 March revealed the degree of politicisation of the Army. The said manifesto invoked the aspirations of the African peoples to decide their own destiny and also demanded the democratisation of the Portuguese institutions.

From a French perspective, the young officers' aspirations were supported by Costa Gomes and Spínola, and Caetano dismissed the two generals in the face of pressure from the ultras, opening a crisis that led to the Caldas revolt on 16 March. Although it was a failed coup, according to certain rumours, it was part of a wider plan, which was foiled at the last moment. After a wave of arrests and purges, the Caldas da Rainha mutiny first resulted in a hardening of the regime. Even so, despite the unrest in the universities and the activity of opposition movements, order reigned in Portugal, as far as the French were concerned. Moreover, the exercise of power was largely facilitated by a depoliticization of the masses, who remained totally indifferent in the face of the March events. However, the repression did not seem to have reassured the army, as a new clandestine manifesto even indicated a hardening of the captains, although the call for rebellion may have meant that extremist elements were seeking to exploit the situation. Even if the officers were not, for the most part, disposed to revolt, the state of mind that animated them no longer made it possible to consider that the Army remained the regime's main support in maintaining the war. It was therefore doubtful that a recovery would be enough to restore the internal front, tirelessly presented by the regime as the only condition for final victory. Whatever the appearances, the immobility of Portuguese political life was truly broken, concluded the note from the Southern Europe sub-directorate.[12]

Caught by Surprise

It seemed that nobody at PIDE/DGS knew that the coup would take place on the night of 24–25 April. Former PIDE/DGS inspector Cunha Passo, who in Portugal also headed the national Interpol office, was at a NATO meeting in Brussels on the day of the revolution and confessed that they were not expecting a coup until May. He went to Brussels with Barbieri Cardoso, the second most important figure in the political police, who was also surprised by the coup, but already in Paris, where he went to meet Alexandre de Marenches, the head of the French secret service.[13] A different opinion is that of the former Deputy Inspector Abílio Augusto Pires, who stated that on the eve of the coup he was at the headquarters of the political police and that he suspected that something was going to happen, given that the day beforehand some soldiers had gone to get radio equipment from the Cascais barracks. He also mentioned that the Under-Secretary of State for the Army, Viana de Lemos, always dismissed the possibility of a military coup, saying that if that was the case, his brother-in-law – Colonel Romeiras Júnior of Cavalry 7 – would solve everything in an instant.[14] Another PIDE/DGS operative, Óscar Cardoso, also stated that the political police knew that 25 April would happen, since after the coup of Caldas, on 16 March, the PIDE controlled 'all the movements of the subversive

After the Caldas revolt, Otelo was never under the surveillance of the political police and managed to act without being detected. He was thus free to prepare the order of operations that led to the coup that ended the regime. (Giorgio Piredda/Sygma/Getty Images)

Headquarters of the political police in Lisbon. The April coup was a surprise to the PIDE/DGS, which did not foresee that the military were preparing a coup to overthrow the regime. (Miranda Castela collection/Archive of the Assembly of the Republic)

military.'[15] It is natural that the political police had, at that moment, several military figures under surveillance, but clearly did not control the most important ones, as was the case of Otelo.

Moreover, these testimonies, as to the date of the coup, contradict the fact that Barbieri Cardoso himself was surprised in Paris, in Marenches' office, by the coup in Lisbon. As deputy director of the political police, Barbieri was certainly well informed about what was happening in the country, but he was astonished when Marenches told him that a revolution was taking place in Portugal. The head of the French secret service reported that Barbieri could not believe what he had just heard and that they even tried calling his office in Lisbon, but only heard noises and buzzing.[16] 'The revolution (…) came effectively by surprise' and was conducted efficiently – confessed Marcello Caetano, later, in his Brazilian exile.[17]

In fact, the order of operations was prepared by Otelo in great secrecy and, besides the seizure of power in Lisbon, it had missions assigned to more than two dozen units spread throughout the country. But it was in the capital that Otelo needed to have a blazing victory and for that it was necessary to neutralise the army units quartered in Lisbon that could be on the government's side and cause problems for the movement's forces. One way to achieve this was to neutralise their commanders through commando-type special forces actions that would quickly arrest the most influential officers of the forces loyal to the government. Otelo had no one to do this and he entrusted this mission to Major Jaime Neves, known to be a fearless officer with experience in commanding special forces, although his performance did not meet Otelo's expectations.[18] In fact, Jaime Neves was unable to form a group of military personnel capable of executing such missions and it had to be Otelo who recruited the military personnel necessary to carry out the missions in question.

In its operations plan, the strategist of 25 April, divided the country into two zones: north of the Douro River, where the forces loyal to the movement should converge on Porto to help the forces quartered in this city to take the objectives set out in the general plan of operations and also garrison the northern and north-eastern borders of the country; as for the rest of Portugal, the forces of the movement should converge on Lisbon and other points where there were regional objectives to take, and garrison the eastern border with Spain. All these forces were to be controlled from a central Command Post (*Posto de Comando*, PC) located in Lisbon, where the MFA officers responsible for the operation would be located.[19] Otelo had at his disposal a small army of 5,000 men to carry out the coup, and of this contingent 3,000 were to converge on Lisbon.[20]

The order of operations show that Otelo had foreseen the involvement of 27 units from various parts of the country that would take positions in various locations to ensure the success of the coup.[21] Also important in this context were the communications between the Command Post and the various units that were in the charge of Lieutenant Colonel Garcia dos Santos, who at the time was a professor of Transmission Tactics at the Military Academy. It was in this institution that Garcia dos Santos 'diverted' communications material to be used in the military uprising. These included the Racal TR-28 transmitter-receivers of South African origin that were already in use in Africa and, therefore, well known by the military personnel and that would be distributed to the intervening units that did not have this type of equipment. Otelo also felt the need to have a radio and telephone link with the Military Telecommunications Service (*Serviço de Transmissões Militares*, STM), which was installed at the Transmission Practice School (*Escola Prática de Transmissões*, EPT) in Lisbon, and which ensured all permanent links between Army units. Besides the STM, the EPT also housed the National Transmission Centre (*Centro Nacional de Transmissões*, CNT), which controlled all the military communications of the Ministry of Defence and the Army, as well as the connections with the security forces, PIDE/DGS, and the Portuguese Legion. Garcia dos Santos was also an instructor at the EPT and knew the communications officers well. He found out that the installation of a telephone cable between the STM and the Military College was planned, which led him to take advantage of the situation and to clandestinely extend the cable from the Military College to the Regiment of Engineering No1 in Pontinha, where the movement's PC would be installed. This point-to-point connection was ready on the afternoon of 24 April between the PC and the STM, and Otelo gained at that moment the ability to communicate with all the military units involved in the coup.

Another concern of Otelo and Garcia dos Santos was to set up at the EPT, with the complicity of officers of that unit, a permanent listening service to the radio networks of the security forces, PIDE/DGS, and Portuguese Legion, and to the telephone conversations of the Minister of Defence, the Army, and the Army Chief of Staff, using for that purpose the CNT. In this way, this whole system of connection to the PC in Pontinha, allowed the MFA officers responsible for the operation to follow in real time the progression of the movement's forces and, at the same time, to know the intentions of the opposing forces and of the government itself through the

Garcia dos Santos (with glasses) in the 1980s when he was Chief of Staff of the Army. In the April revolution, he played a very important role in the MFA's communications, setting up a network that allowed the Command Post in Pontinha to monitor government communications and communicate with the units involved in the coup. (National Defence Archive)

João Paulo Dinis, the man responsible for issuing the first codeword in the form of a song on the radio on the night of 24 April. (Carlos Coelho da Silva collection)

Otelo Saraiva de Carvalho once again played an important role in the preparation of the military coup, by convincing João Paulo Dinis to broadcast the first codeword on the radio to the units in Lisbon. (Carlos Coelho da Silva collection)

bugging service, which was a fundamental factor for the success of the coup.[22]

On the night of 22 April, Otelo was meeting at Jaime Neves' flat in Reboleira, Lisbon, with Captain Morais da Silva and some of the elements that would arrest the opposing officers, a group that had been mobilised by Captain Rui Rodrigues, at the Infantry Practical School of Mafra, where Rodrigues was serving. At the request of Costa Martins, an Air Force pilot that Otelo had nominated to control the Portuguese Radio Club (*Rádio Clube Português*, RCP), Otelo went to meet with João Paulo Dinis, whom he knew from his time in Guinea and who worked at the radio station. João Paulo had already been approached by Costa Martins but had become suspicious and wanted to speak directly to Otelo. Thus, Otelo went to meet him with Costa Martins and Major Costa Neves, another Air Force officer who was part of the group in charge of the RCP assault and who did not know João Paulo Dinis. Otelo told Dinis that he needed someone at the RCP to ensure the transmission of a radio signal that would reach the whole country, warning the elements of the movement of the start of the coup. However, João Paulo told him that he was not the one doing the news at dawn and that he did not really work at RCP, but at a production company from Lisbon (Productions Alfabeta), which had rented a room at RCP to broadcast João Paulo's programme on the radio, which ended at midnight. Otelo then asked him to find out who was the man on duty at RCP on the night of the 24–25 April. Later that night, João Paulo Dinis told him that the journalist on duty at the radio would be Joaquim Furtado, but that he did not know whether or not they could count on him. Otelo also found out that RCP had a low power output, covering only the city of Lisbon and, at most, 100 kilometres around it. That was when he decided to broadcast two signals. A first one given by João Paulo Dinis and destined for the units of the Lisbon area, which from that signal would start the preparations inside the barracks, and a second signal that would be broadcasted by *Rádio Renascença* for the whole country, for the remaining units that were waiting.

The song that Paulo de Carvalho took to the Eurovision festival and that served as the first codeword to trigger the April revolution. (José Matos collection)

Radio Signals

That year, the singer Paulo de Carvalho had won the Portuguese television song festival and represented the country at the Eurovision Song Contest in Brighton, in the UK, with the song *E depois do Adeus*. Being a popular song, which would not arouse suspicion, it was chosen to serve as the first radio signal to the troops of the movement: it was five minutes to 11pm on 24 April, when Paulo de Carvalho's voice signalled to the military units in Lisbon that they could start the preparations for the seizure of power.

On *Rádio Renascença*, close to half past midnight, the first verse of the song *Grândola, Vila Morena* by José Afonso would be read and then the complete song would be heard. The second signal confirmed that the coup was under way and that the situation was irreversible. The song was chosen by Almada Contreiras, a naval

The occupation of the RTP television studios was a priority in Otelo's plans and took place peacefully. (A Capital)

officer, who was a friend of José Afonso and who thought the song was very beautiful.[23]

The movement decided to take up positions with the RCP, defending the station from any incursion by the forces of order, a position that was deemed unnecessary for the case of *Rádio Renascença*.[24]

Portuguese television (*Rádio Televisão Portuguesa*, Radio Television Portugal, RTP) was also an important target to conquer, and the operations were in charge of EPAM (*Escola Prática de Administração Militar*, Military Administration Practical School), which had its facilities near the RTP studios. The force that would

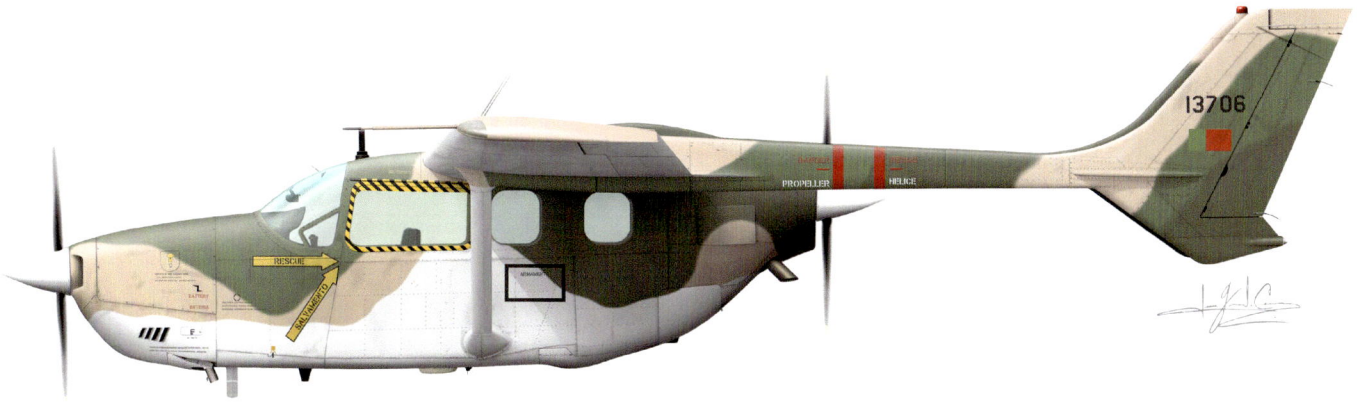

The incessant pace of operations maintained by the FAP's Do-27 fleet in Africa resulted in maintenance difficulties and flight safety issues, prompting the search for a replacement. Portugal settled on the Reims-Cessna FTB-337G Milirole, produced in France and conveniently marketed as a civil aircraft. The first Milirole arrived at Tancos Air Base Nº 3 (BA3) in December 1974, after the war had ended, but were quickly distributed to other units. Initially they sported an anti-radiation olive-green colour scheme, but from 1981 onwards they carried a camouflage pattern in two-tone brown and green. (Artwork by Luca Canossa)

In February 1974, Portugal ordered 28 C-212 Aviocar transport aircraft from the Spanish company CASA. The order was later reduced to 24 aircraft, but the war had ended by the time the first Aviocar arrived in Portugal in October 1974. The Aviocars were initially assigned to Esquadra 32 at Air Base No. 3 (BA3) in Tancos, a former Noratlas unit given the mission of adapting Portuguese crews to the new aircraft. This Aviocar had an anti-radiation olive-green paint scheme, but from the 1980s onwards they were given a camouflage of brown and two shades of green. (Artwork by Luca Canossa)

The Mirage 5, produced by Dassault in the early 1970s, was an attack fighter powered by the SNECMA Atar 09C-3 engine. Specifically designed for air-to-ground roles, the Mirage 5 lacked the Cyrano II radar carried by the Mirage III, but its wide range of weapons and simplified maintenance made it a great export success. The Mirage 5 was Lisbon's initial choice to re-equip the Portuguese Air Force (FAP) with a supersonic combat aircraft, and several contacts were made between Portugal and France to buy the Dassault fighter, but a lack of funds delayed the purchase. It was not until 1974 that Portugal obtained a South African loan to buy 32 Mirage IIIEPL fighters – a version specifically tailored to Portugal's needs – but efforts to conclude the sale were halted after 25 April. (Artworks by Tom Cooper)

Despite the fact that the vast majority of officers on 25 April preferred flashier uniforms, Captain Salgueiro Maia, commander of the column coming from the Practical Cavalry School in Santarém, preferred to wear the same uniform as his troops, i.e., the olive-green No. 2 service kit, consisting of a shirt with chest pockets and trousers with large side pockets. The three stripes on the shoulders demonstrate the simple and clear way the Portuguese found to differentiate their officers. Although this officer previously led commando units in Guinea-Bissau, the only badge or qualification insignia he wears is that of the armoured troops, attached just above the left pocket. On his shoulder is the ubiquitous 7.62 mm NATO calibre G3 assault rifle, in this case equipped with a 10x sniper scope. (Artwork by Anderson Subtil)

A Special Marine, certainly a veteran of the fighting overseas, as seen on the streets of Lisbon on 25 April 1974. Despite being an infantryman, he is wearing the same black uniform as Portuguese sailors, but with the addition of the Marines' black beret and their qualification badges. Some photos show marines in full combat gear, but in this case our subject is only wearing a canvas belt and two sets of regulation magazine pouches. The uniform is completed by waterproof boots without laces, suitable for amphibious action, and individual weaponry consisting of the reliable and widely used MG-42/59 machine gun in 7.62 mm NATO calibre. (Artwork by Anderson Subtil)

CARNATION REVOLUTION VOLUME 2: COUP IN PORTUGAL, APRIL 1974

A serviceman from the former Portuguese Air Force (FAP) Parachute Regiment drinks a cup of coffee given to him by a passer-by, probably on the outskirts of Lisbon airport. The attire of this member of the Lusitanian airborne elite includes reinforced boots, suitable for parachute jumping, and the regiment's characteristic green beret, a local exclusive, since most other Western airborne forces, influenced by the Americans and the British, prefer to wear red or grey. The uniform is based on the French 1950 model, but the dolman and trousers are different variations on the Portuguese 'lizard' pattern. Note the paratroopers' magazine pouches, simpler in design than those used by the regular infantry, and the holster for the 9mm Parabellum Luger. The large black leather pouch is probably carrying a first aid kit and his rifle is a G3 in its folding-stock version (Artwork by Anderson Subtil)

This junior officer from Regiment No. 7, one of the few units mobilised by the regime to counter the rebels, is wearing the characteristic clothing of Portuguese officers serving in the metropolis in the 1970s, including a green shirt and tie and an elegant leather jacket with the rank badges attached to the shoulder flaps. The cavalry trousers and long spurred boots were items unique to cavalry officers. He also wears a model M40 steel helmet, although most cavalrymen active during the military coup preferred the black beret, adorned with the cavalry's badge of crossed sabres, topped by the regimental number. His pistol is a classic Walther P38 and his submachine gun a Portuguese-designed FBP, much used in the Overseas War, both weapons in 9mm Parabellum calibre. (Artwork by Anderson Subtil)

Portugal purchased 50 Panhard EBR 75 (*Engin Blindé de Reconnaissance*) armoured cars from France in 1959. Each of these vehicles possessed a 75mm cannon as well as three 7.5mm machine guns. Twenty-one were deployed to Angola (Luanda and Silva Porto where this example served with *Dragoes de Angola*), while the rest were stationed in mainland Portugal with Army cavalry units. During the April 1974 revolution, the Cavalry Practical School from Santarém sent three of these vehicles to Lisbon, where they were used in city centre operations and the siege of the Carmo barracks. (Artwork by David Bocquelet)

The Panhard ETT (*Engin Transporteur de Troupes*) was a specialised vehicle variant produced exclusively for Portugal. Comparable to the EBR in many respects, the ETT also had a passenger compartment for 14 soldiers and carried a single turret-mounted 7.62mm machine gun. Just one of these vehicles accompanied Salgueiro Maia's column from Santarém to Lisbon on 25 April, although additional ETTs, assigned to other units, also travelled to Lisbon to support the coup. (Artwork by David Bocquelet)

The Portuguese Army purchased 40 Panhard AML-60 armoured patrol cars from France in the mid-1960s. They were soon serving in Angola, Mozambique, and Guinea, as well as with the Practical Cavalry School and Cavalry regiments on the mainland. Equipped with a 60mm gun-mortar and two 7.62mm machine guns, each AML-60 carried three soldiers and could reach speeds up to 90km/h. Later in the decade Portugal obtained 32 Eland-60s, a South African derivative of the AML family, as a result of Pretoria's growing willingness to assist Portugal's cause in Africa. Several of these vehicles from Santarém and Cavalry Regiment 7 participated in the events of 25 April 1974, in Lisbon. (Artwork by David Bocquelet)

In 1974, the National Republican Guard (GNR) was expecting the delivery of 38 Shorland Mark III armoured patrol vehicles. Originally designed for use by the Royal Ulster Constabulary in Northern Ireland, the Shorland was essentially a Land Rover with Makrolon armour plate protecting the body and rear from small arms fire. This vehicle sported a single 7.62mm FN MAG machine gun but was primarily designed for riot control; for that purpose, it was fitted with smoke and tear gas grenade launchers. The Shorland posed a potential threat to the coup planners, since the GNR was favourable to the regime. On 25 April, however, the GNR had only three functional vehicles available, and those were unarmed. (Artwork by David Bocquelet)

In 1970 the Portuguese Army received its first Chaimite, a small armoured personnel transport vehicle with 4x4 traction developed and manufactured in Portugal, although based on the US Cadillac Gage Commando V-100. The Chaimite saw action in Africa as a reconnaissance and troop transport platform, and surviving examples served in the Portuguese Army until 2016. Its use by the Practical Cavalry School from Santarém became well-known, particularly for its involvement in the events of the April revolution in 1974. The deposed head of the overthrown regime, Marcello Caetano, was driven from the Carmo barracks to the rebel troops' operations centre in Pontinha in a Chaimite vehicle called *Bula*. (Artwork by David Bocquelet)

The introduction of the M47 Patton medium tanks in 1952 provided a significant boost to the mechanisation of the Portuguese Cavalry. The first tank squadrons were established at Campo Militar de Santa Margarida while crew training was assigned to the Cavalry Practical School, then based in Torres Novas. In 1974, four M47s were transferred from Santa Margarida to Cavalry Regiment 7 in Lisbon, opposite Salgueiro Maia's troops in Terreiro do Paço, and ended up joining the revolutionaries. The Patton could reach a top speed of 48km/h and was equipped with a 90mm M36 cannon. (Artwork by David Bocquelet)

After the revolution, the Communist Party of Portugal quickly attracted lots of sympathisers within the armed forces. Here, they can be seen gathering around an AML-60 armoured car. (José Matos collection)

One of the Shorland Mk 3s of the National Guard, acquired in 1974. At the time of the April revolution only three vehicles were operational, and they posed no threat to the MFA troops. (Pedro Monteiro collection)

A Chaimite V-200 armoured car of the Portuguese Army. Produced in Portugal this armoured troop transport vehicle was based on the American Cadillac Gage V-100. (Pedro Monteiro collection)

Portuguese soldiers during the Carnation Revolution in Lisbon, 25 April 1974. (Jean-Claude Francolon/Gamma-Rapho via Getty Images)

(Map by Tom Cooper)

Portuguese marines in Mozambique during the colonial war. During the preparation of the coup, Otelo ensured the neutrality of these special forces to avoid interference with the MFA forces. (Ben Martin/Getty Images)

take over the television studios was commanded by Captain Teófilo Bento, who, despite being a logistics officer, that is, of a non-combatant force, performed his mission well.[25]

On the night of 21 April, Otelo did not get the support of the paratroopers, but was assured of their neutrality. That night he met the commander of the paratroopers, Colonel Fausto Marques, but quickly realised that Fausto Marques was too cautious and raised several doubts about the preparation of the operation, however, he received a guarantee that the paratroopers would not take any action against the forces of the movement.[26] In the same vein, he managed to obtain the neutrality of the Marines. At a meeting at the home of Commander Vítor Crespo, who was a Marine, the commanders of the Marines assured Otelo that they would not intervene either.[27]

In this way, Otelo guaranteed the neutrality of the special forces, which in fact would not intervene in any way on the day of the revolution. Another concern of the coup strategist was the Portuguese Air Force (*Força Aérea Portuguesa*, FAP), which could obviously intervene against the forces of the movement. However, Otelo had guarantees from various pilots that they would not accept orders to 'take part in bombing actions over Lisbon or over provincial units occupied' by the MFA troops.[28] Moreover, the start of operations would take place during the early hours of the morning, as the FAP did not have the capacity to act during the night.

Costa Gomes was the MFA's favourite to assume the Presidency of the Republic after the coup, but it was Spínola who ended up occupying the post. (Revista do Povo collection)

Three days before 'H-hour', Otelo could only count practically on the Army as 'friendly' forces, and he managed to get a significant number of garrisons from all over the country to join him. In Lisbon, only two units were considered hostile to the movement: the RC7 and the RL2. But the Regiment of Infantry 1 (RI1), from Amadora, eventually withdrew in the middle of the night of 24 April, when Otelo was already at the Command Post in Pontinha. The RI1 had the mission of assaulting and occupying the fort at Caxias to release political prisoners and arrest the DGS agents that were there, and also to ensure the safety of generals Costa Gomes and Spínola. In light of this, the movement took the risk of not launching an attack on the fort at Caxias, nor on the DGS headquarters, which should also have been occupied by the forces of this regiment. To the south, RI4 of Faro also gave notice, on 19 April of its non-alignment in the coup. Otelo also recorded problems in Évora, where the headquarters commanding the whole south of the country was located. In the north, he mentioned the importance that Dinis de Almeida's transfer from RAL 5 in Penafiel to RAP 3 (Heavy Artillery Regiment 3) in Figueira da Foz had for the movement as a form of punishment. There he militated for the movement in Aveiro, Águeda, Coimbra and Figueira da Foz. Those were dizzying days with continuous contacts and meetings to motivate and mobilise troops and to prepare for the functions to be performed on 25 April.[29] But on the eve of the coup, Otelo was confident that he had the numbers of troops and units sufficient to dominate the situation.

On the political side of the movement, Vítor Alves coordinated the team responsible for the political programme that was practically concluded on 20 April, as well as the terms of a secret protocol to be agreed between the National Salvation Junta (*Junta de Salvação Nacional*, JSN) and the MFA (which was never signed) and the text of the MFA proclamation to the country that would be read over the microphones of *Rádio Clube Português*. The working group was formed by men from the Army, the Navy, and the Air Force, but the latter was conspicuous by its absence, and it was only at the decisive meeting, on the 20th, that Major Morais da Silva appeared to speak on behalf of the FAP and raised several doubts as to the programme's content, especially the part concerning the self-determination of the colonies.[30] However, the program was practically closed and the final preparations for the coup were irreversible.

Otelo was one of Spínola's liaison elements and in the month of April he continued to play this role but using another third element for fear that Spínola was being watched by PIDE/DGS. He used Carlos Alexandre de Morais, who was Spínola's daily visitor and whom Otelo knew from Guinea, thus avoiding any suspicion. It was Carlos Morais who brought Spínola the first version of the MFA political programme and he returned it two days later with his questions, corrections and disagreements written in pencil. It is clear that the general had some reservations regarding certain terms

Costa Gomes always kept a certain distance from the MFA during the preparation of the coup, avoiding any participation in it. In his opinion, the military uprising should have taken place in the African colonies and not in Portugal. (Revista do Povo collection)

Kenneth Kaunda with President Costa Gomes at Lisbon airport in 1975, during a visit by the President of Zambia to Portugal. In 1973, Kaunda had contacts with Jorge Jardim to mediate a solution to the war in Mozambique that included the independence of the colony, the so-called Lusaka Memorandum. But the plan was never accepted by Marcello Caetano. (AEI)

Costa Gomes and Vasco Gonçalves in October 1974, at the beginning of the second provisional government led by Vasco Gonçalves. Before the revolution, Vasco Gonçalves was the liaison officer between the MFA and Costa Gomes. (Revista do Povo collection)

used in the document and the type of ideology that inspired it.[31] Carlos Morais made three or four trips with the document between Spínola and the movement. Spínola agreed to join the JSN – the designation he himself had proposed – under the terms expressed in the documents. In this context, it was initially decided that the JSN would be made up of six general officers, two from the Army, two from the Navy and two from the Air Force (later one more element was added to be the provisional President of the Republic). On the part of the Army both Spínola and Costa Gomes guaranteed (the latter through Vasco Gonçalves) their presence in the JSN. The preference of the MFA officers was for Costa Gomes to be the President of the Republic and Spínola the CEMGFA, but on the day of the revolution, Spínola would end up taking the leading role by receiving Marcello Caetano's surrender.[32]

While Carlos Morais played this role with Spínola, Vasco Gonçalves did the same with Costa Gomes, but without any success regarding the involvement of this general in the conspiracy. Costa Gomes always kept a certain distance in relation to the MFA, avoiding compromising himself. Spínola himself visited Costa Gomes on 14 April to talk to him about the MFA programme and the changes he had proposed, but Costa Gomes refused to take note of the political programme and advised Spínola not to commit himself to the MFA. In Costa Gomes's opinion, a military revolt should have been unleashed in the Overseas Territories and not in the mainland, where it risked ending in a 'bloodbath,' and in this sense, he thought the military coup being prepared by the MFA was a bad idea.[33]

Costa Gomes would later state that he only learned of the MFA programme eight days before 25 April (18 April?) and that it was shown to him by a commission made up of officers, including Colonel Vasco Gonçalves, who had served with him in Mozambique and Angola. 'Of all the elements that made up the coordinating commission, he was really the officer who had the most contact with me.'[34] Costa Gomes also mentioned that his telephone was tapped in March 1974, following his refusal to participate in the ceremony of loyalty to Marcello Caetano, and armed elements of the PIDE were placed in a building adjacent to his, with two cars always in the vicinity, which followed him everywhere. When asked if it was common for officers to be watched by the PIDE, Costa Gomes replied 'especially those whom the PIDE distrusted for political or religious reasons.'[35] These statements by Costa Gomes show that the political police were probably watching the two generals after their dismissal in March. The question is, by whose orders?[36]

On 18 April, Otelo met Major Alexandre Aragão in the street. He should have been in Guinea but had come to Lisbon to meet with Spínola. The meeting with Otelo took place after Aragão had spoken to the general, who told him: 'That he was completely unaware of what was happening regarding the outbreak of the military coup, but he was sure that something was being prepared soon.' Alexandre Aragão was head of the militia section at the Headquarters of the Armed Forces Command in Guinea and told Otelo that in Bissau there was a plan prepared to launch a coup in Guinea and end the war in that colony. From the conversation with Otelo it was agreed that if the coup failed in Lisbon, the MFA would launch military action in Guinea against the ruling power.[37] That same night, Otelo held a decisive meeting at his home in Oeiras with officers from various units of the Lisbon Military Region to inform them of the various objectives and the missions that each unit would perform.[38]

Unaware of these manoeuvres, Marcello Caetano received Jorge Jardim at his private residence on 17 April. Jorge Jardim had come from Mozambique to present the President of the Council with the 'Lusaka Programme,' which Jardim had negotiated directly with Zambia's President Kenneth Kaunda.

Jardim had been in contact with the Zambian leader since July 1973, defending a political solution for Mozambique that included the future independence of the territory.[39] These contacts were Jardim's personal initiative without consulting Lisbon and denoted his own agenda, which was not exactly the same as Caetano's. The head of government obviously had no intention of giving independence to Mozambique, contrary to Jardim's wishes. Moreover, Caetano was receiving information from Mozambique through other channels and was beginning to distrust Jardim's intentions. On 17 April, Jardim presented him with the Lusaka Memorandum and tried to convince Marcello that this was the solution to the war. The program, which had been negotiated by Jardim more than half a year earlier, advocated a move away from Portugal in relation to South Africa and Rhodesia, which were hostile states for the achievement of peace from the Zambian perspective, and argued that the independence of the Portuguese territories in Africa was the only possible solution to end the war there. The memorandum also argued that the Portuguese regime should recognise nationalist movements that could not be ignored in the formation of future independent states.[40] Caetano obviously could not accept any of this and realised that Jardim had gone too far in his contacts with Zambia.[41] It seems clear that Jardim was unaware of the true dimension of the cooperation with South Africa and Rhodesia and of the commitments Portugal had already undertaken with these countries within the Alcora alliance, which allowed the Portuguese regime to finance the war and obtain military aid.

After the Carnation Revolution, there were also rumours that Marcello Caetano had given instructions to the Angolan governor, Fernando Santos e Castro, to stir up a process of independence in Angola, which would involve a rupture with the mainland. Santos e Castro came to Lisbon in February 1974, and it was allegedly during this visit that Caetano instructed him on his return to Luanda to create conditions to foment a nationalist wave that would lead to the breaking off of relations with Portugal and the unilateral declaration of independence planned for 15 August 1974. The future government of Angola would not be solely white, but multiracial with the participation of Jonas Savimbi. This question had been raised by former collaborators of Fernando Santos e Castro in the colonial administration.[42] There is no document from this period in Marcello Caetano's archive that indicates such an intention, there being only information about the visit that Marcello intended to make to the two southern colonies in May 1974 and which could be used to announce some important measures, although there is no information about this.[43] The issue has provoked controversy over time, but it does not seem plausible that the President of the Council was interested in promoting abrupt independence for Angola when at the same time he was preparing to prolong the war with South African support. In his mind, Angola could become independent within two or three years, but never in 1974.[44] Furthermore, there are testimonies that contradict this thesis, such as that of Soares Carneiro, who was secretary-general of the Angolan government in Santos e Castro's time and who never heard the governor speak of such a hypothesis.[45]

Although he did not reveal everything in his writings, Marcello Caetano seems never to have had a genuine will to truly negotiate with the liberation movements, which for him were at the service of

Angola's Governor, Fernando Santos e Castro, at a public ceremony in the city of Lobito. There are some reports that Santos e Castro received instructions from Marcello Caetano to lead Angola's independence. (AHU)

Marcello Caetano with Sir Alec Douglas-Home, the UK Foreign Secretary at the Foreign Office, during a visit he made to London in July 1973. Although British diplomacy facilitated contacts with the PAIGC in the British capital in 1974, Caetano never showed much interest in negotiating independence with the guerrillas. (Press Association photo)

foreign powers and wanted to expel the whites from Africa.[46] Even the contacts in London with elements of the PAIGC, facilitated by British diplomacy, were nothing more than a delaying tactic to gain time, while the regime did not have the weapons it wanted. Caetano was committed to a progressive autonomy of the colonies and to the creation of an African elite that could progressively take control of the territories, but without involving the guerrilla leaders. This can be seen in the help he sought from the French, who were available to mediate a negotiated solution for Guinea.

The French View

The French availability had been expressed to the Portuguese Minister of Foreign Affairs, Rui Patrício, during his visit to France in January 1974. The Portuguese minister's visit had been carefully prepared by French diplomats, who anticipated that Patrício would appeal to the old ties between the two countries to ask France for a more collaborative attitude in votes at the United Nations and also permission to sell war material (Mirage fighters and helicopters), two areas in which the French had already been, over the last decade, as understanding as their African policy allowed. In an internal note from the Directorate of African and Malagasy Affairs (DAM) on the minister's visit, it was clearly stated that the complaints and international pressures against Portugal had worsened, and therefore that to waive the restrictions in place or agree to sell new war material, such as the Mirage for example, would risk opening a crisis in French relations with Africa. Moreover, Patrício was coming to Paris at a 'difficult time' for Portugal, which would be reason enough for the French to suggest 'ways out of the impasse' caused by the war, telling him clearly that the best way was negotiation. However, for DAM, the question of Angola and Mozambique should be separated from Guinea. The two southern provinces had in common great natural wealth and relatively important white institutions, unlike Guinea-Bissau, which was a territory with no economic value, almost no settlers and in a difficult military situation for Portuguese troops. In this context, it was natural that Portugal wanted to keep Angola and Mozambique, where the military situation was more under control. DAM also considered that, at this stage, it could not be excluded that the Portuguese regime would seek an 'honourable way out' of Guinea, but for this to happen, two conditions were necessary: the first was that there should be no talk of the independence of Angola and Mozambique and the second that the fate of the Cape Verde archipelago should be separated from the Guinea independence process, believing that this last requirement, could be admitted by the PAIGC leaders, who had made no reference to Cape Verde in the unilateral declaration of independence of Guinea-Bissau in September 1973. DAM also recognised that it was because of the war in Guinea that the Portuguese caused the most embarrassment to French diplomacy, due to the privileged relations that France had with Senegal. Whenever incidents occurred on the border between Guinea and Senegal, Paris was in a very delicate situation vis-à-vis its former colony. It was therefore clear that the problem of Guinea had to be resolved at the negotiating table, which could be mediated by President Senghor, and that France could 'facilitate, once again, the Luso-Senegalese dialogue.'[47]

It was in this context that Rui Patrício landed in Paris on 7 January 1974, and was confronted with the French view on Portuguese policy in Africa. Patrício met Michel Jobert, the French Minister of Foreign Affairs, who warned his Portuguese counterpart that Portugal was becoming increasingly isolated on the international scene and that something had to be done urgently to change this. France did not want to create difficulties for Portugal, but however rather to help defend a policy for Africa that it did not want to compromise, and which was not exactly the same as Portugal's. Jobert gave Brazil as an example, which he considered to be a Portuguese success story, and asked why not do the same in Angola and Mozambique? In the minister's opinion, confederal autonomy would be a good way of calming world public opinion and would give time to create solid entities. As for Guinea-Bissau, Jobert also hoped that Portugal would adopt a different colonial policy (supposedly more open to dialogue and negotiation), which would also allow France to advocate a confederal solution, but 'if Portugal does not want to leave its system, that will be a big problem for us,' the French minister confessed. Patrício replied by saying that 'it has been wrongly underlined that there is an opposition between Portugal's African policy on the one hand, and that of France and Great Britain on the other.' For the Portuguese minister, Portugal had no choice but to maintain the policy it had been following, 'if we do not want to brutally destroy the historical basis of the Portuguese presence in Africa.' On the federal question, the Portuguese colonies were already in a way federal states with great autonomy (since the revision of the organic law of Overseas Territories in 1972) although Patrício could not say so publicly. However, Portugal was promoting a policy of great economic development in Angola and Mozambique and also the Africanisation of the military. Although Patrício never

Michel Jobert, in his office in Paris, where talks were reportedly held with the Portuguese minister Rui Patrício in 1974. Jobert advised Patrício to have a policy in Africa that was more open to dialogue and negotiation with the liberation movements. (Svenskt Pressphoto/Bild-Arkiv)

spoke of future independent states, in his opinion, an evolution towards a multiracial community of Portuguese culture could be expected in the long term, but would always be a gradual, long-term process.[48] Patrício's arguments clearly showed the difficulty in accepting any kind of negotiated solution for Guinea and by extension for the remaining colonies.

After the meeting between the heads of Luso-French diplomacy, Freitas Cruz, who was the Director-General of Political Affairs and who was accompanying the minister, had a meeting with his French counterpart, taking with him a paper that Patrício had passed to him about the previous session. At this meeting, Freitas Cruz confessed to his counterpart that the minister appreciated the frankness and friendly clarity of the French opinions and that he reacted with interest to the presentation that was made. He assured that on the 'Portuguese side we will reflect' because it was clear to him that it was necessary to find a new presentation of Portuguese policy vis-à-vis the international community. On the French side, the impression was that the minister had not reacted unfavourably to the idea of talks on Guinea, but on this subject, there could be no illusions: even with French help, talks with the most moderate African governments would lead to nothing if, at some point, no contact was made with the PAIGC leadership. Regarding this possibility, Freitas Cruz argued that a Portuguese, non-governmental, non-official personality could be found who could carry out this task in a discreet manner, not directly involving the Portuguese State. Still on this subject, Freitas Cruz recalled recent contacts that had been established by the Portuguese ambassador in Bonn and his Zambian colleague, but when the Zambian ambassador invited the Portuguese ambassador to lunch with a representative of a liberation movement, the latter had to decline, and the matter remained unresolved. Having said this, Freitas Cruz did not rule out the possibility that something could be done in this direction and that, in this situation, the support of France could be precious to Portugal and, if this step was taken, he would come especially to Paris to speak with his counterpart.[49]

Three months after this round of talks, Marcello Caetano sent a special representative to the French capital, Pedro Feytor Pinto from the Secretariat of State for Information and Tourism, to meet with Jacques Foccart, President Pompidou's advisor on African affairs, and Jean Mourichaud-Beaupré, who had been ambassador to some African countries. His instructions were in line with what had been said in January, that was, to enlist the support of more moderate African political leaders, such as Senghor in Senegal or Houphouet-Boigny in Côte d'Ivoire, who would help the Portuguese in a solution of gradual autonomy, slower but less violent than an abrupt independence.[50] Marcello's envoy arrived in Paris on 5 April and was well received by his interlocutors, but as the French were well informed about the internal situation in Portugal, they were going to wait and see, although they would not fail to establish the necessary contacts and would inform Feytor Pinto. However, it was evident in this approach that Marcello Caetano did not want to negotiate directly with the liberation movements that wanted immediate independence.

There were also contacts in Italy between the press officer at the Portuguese embassy, Mário Matos e Lemos, and the MPLA representative in Italy, Manuel Jorge. These contacts were authorised in part by Moreira Baptista, when he was Secretary of State for Information and Tourism, with the knowledge of the President of the Council. However, the Press Councillor's instructions were to talk to Italian politicians who could possibly mediate contacts with African movements. Matos e Lemos was not authorised to speak with any representative of these movements. However, when that possibility arose, the question was put to Lisbon to the Ministry of Foreign Affairs and Rui Patrício gave orders that there should be no contact between Matos e Lemos and the representative of the 'terrorist movement.' From the content of the instructions given, it was clear that the Portuguese government was not available to negotiate with the liberation movements dubbed 'terrorists.'[51] However, Matos e Lemos ignored Patrício's orders and even met with Manuel Jorge in Rome, but the meeting was nothing more than an exchange of ideas without any practical consequences. Meanwhile, in Portugal, the regime was hanging by a thread.

On the night of 18 April, Américo Thomaz and Marcello Caetano still went to the São Carlos theatre to see the first of three performances (the others were on 21 and 24 April) of Joan Sutherland singing *La Traviata*, recalled the Portuguese poet, writer, and essayist Eduardo Pitta. By chance, Otelo had also bought tickets to go and see this opera on 24 April but ended up giving it up to go and participate in the revolution.[52] Around this time, Marcello Caetano was 'very sad,' his son recalled. Without specifying the date, the President of the Council had already warned the family: 'don't be surprised if something happens.'[53]

In April 1974, Marcello Caetano was visibly tired and had no solutions to the problem of the war in Africa. (José Matos collection)

The Last Council of Ministers

On 23 April, Marcello convened the Council of Ministers for the last time. The meeting dealt mainly with economic issues and the salaries of civil servants, issues that would be dealt with in a future Council of Ministers for Economic Affairs.[54] But the former Minister of the Navy, Pereira Crespo, who was present at the meeting, said that the problem of Overseas Territories was also addressed by Rebelo de Sousa, who was the minister in charge of the sector. The minister drew attention to the need to accelerate the autonomy of the colonies, but reservations were expressed about a possible negative reaction of the Army towards a strengthening of the existing autonomies.[55]

On the evening of that day, Marcello met with his family for the last time in Lisbon for the birthday dinner of a grandson. A few days earlier, Manuel José Homem de Mello, who was a member of the National Assembly, had already noticed that the head of government was not well. At a dinner party at his home in early April attended by Marcello Caetano and several members of the government, Homem de Mello noted that Marcello's physical and moral decline was evident and that he was close to a nervous breakdown. At the end of the dinner, he even said that 'at least we can avoid handing over power to the communists.'[56]

However, despite physical and psychological fatigue, Marcello remained at the head of the government, and the war remained

A French Mirage V with two Sidewinders, two JC 300 combined fuel tank/rocket-launchers, and two 500kg bombs. Initially, the Portuguese were interested in this attack version, but in 1974 they had already opted for the Mirage III because of its air defence capability. (Dassault)

their main concern. On 24 April, unaware of the imminent coup that night, the Minister of Foreign Affairs, Rui Patrício, met with the French ambassador in Lisbon, Bernard Durand, to try to unblock the sale of 32 Mirage III fighter aircraft that the Portuguese government wanted to buy for use in Africa, mainly in Guinea. Initially the Portuguese wanted to buy the Mirage V, the attack version of the famous French fighter, but by 1974 they were clearly leaning towards the Mirage III as it had a greater air defence capability that could be useful against the MiG-17s that were in Conakry.

However, negotiations had already dragged on for several months with the French government demanding that Portugal make a commitment not to move the fighters to Guinea, where they could be used against Senegal, a former French colony with which Paris had privileged relations. It was in Guinea that the Portuguese needed the fighters most, due to the fact that the military situation was the most difficult for the Portuguese troops. In his conversation with the ambassador, Patrício claimed that 'the purchase of the Mirage represented a considerable investment for his country' and that he needed the fighters in Guinea to respond to an air attack coming from Guinea-Conakry, where there were MiG fighters in service. If the Portuguese regime accepted the French restrictions, it would give the impression that it was giving up the defence of Guinea-Bissau, so the restrictions were not acceptable. Bernard Durand argued that Senegal was the problem, and that Portugal had an advantage in having good relations with a moderate African country, but then Patrício suggested that, if necessary, Portugal could give Senegal assurances that no Mirage operations would be conducted against Senegalese territory. The conversation was transmitted to Paris that same day, but it did not have the response that Patrício wanted, as the next day he was no longer minister. But this conversation showed that Portugal urgently needed to buy French aircraft to protect Guinea and give the Air Force more attack capability. If the war continued to escalate in Guinea, the Mirages could easily attack targets in neighbouring countries on retaliatory missions and no neighbouring city would be beyond the range of the French fighters. This new air asset could give the Portuguese a new attack and deterrence capability, but the Mirage would never arrive in Portugal. After the end of the war in Africa, all interest in the new fighter faded.[57] That same day, Patrício attended a reception at the German embassy, where ambassador Ehrenfried von Holleben was organising an event to mark his departure from Portugal, as he was returning to Bonn to retire. The Minister of Defence, Silva Cunha and the Minister of the Interior, Moreira Baptista, were also present. When the latter was asked if the government foresaw any unrest, Moreira Baptista answered no, given that Silva Pais, the director of PIDE/DGS, had been in his office that day and had told him that some unrest could only happen around 1 May, but nothing special, that was, the regime had no idea what was about to happen.[58] Silva Cunha's conversation with Américo Thomaz at the Palácio de Belém on the same day was along the same lines. Thomaz was suspicious that something might happen, due to an alarming letter he had received from Kaúlza de Arriaga a week and a half before. But Silva Cunha was calm and paid little attention to Thomaz's concerns.[59] That night, Patrício had dinner with Jorge Jardim, who was in Lisbon and had been invited by Marcello to be ambassador to Malawi. Also present was ambassador João de Freitas Cruz, who conducted the political affairs of the Ministry of Foreign Affairs. The conversation revolved around the conditions that Jorge Jardim presented to accept the post, but none of those present had any idea what was going to happen that night. It was dawn when Jorge Jardim took Freitas Cruz to the Ministry, where he had left his car. They even

Major Sanches Osório, who was at the Pontinha Command Post together with Otelo in charge of operations. After the coup, he was Minister of Social Communication in the Second Provisional Government, led by Vasco Gonçalves. (M. Valentim/AEI)

Commander Vítor Crespo was the Navy representative at the Pontinha Command Post. After the revolution, he served as High Commissioner in Mozambique. (AEI)

passed by the cipher section to see the latest telegrams received from foreign embassies, but 'there was nothing abnormal or important' and Jardim then went back to the hotel without realising that the revolution was already on the streets.[60]

The Longest Night

Otelo arrived at the Command Post in Pontinha around 10 o'clock in the evening of 24 April. An hour earlier, he had warned Captain António Ramos that the revolution would happen that night and for him to warn General Spínola. Soon after receiving the message, Ramos went to the general's house to tell him that the coup would be unleashed that dawn and that at 3 am an MFA force would arrive in charge of the security of Spínola's house.[61]

At the Command Post, Otelo met Lieutenant Colonel Fisher Lopes Pires, who was the second-in-command of the Engineering Regiment of Pontinha, and Major Sanches Osório. The latter had brought him the movement's communiqués to be read into the radio microphones during the night and early morning of the next day. There was also Garcia dos Santos, in charge of communications, and Captain Luís Macedo, responsible for the security of the Command

Otelo Saraiva de Carvalho with the singer José Afonso, in 1976, when Otelo was a candidate for the Presidency of the Republic. On 24 April 1974, a song by José Afonso was chosen as the second codeword of the revolution. (Associação José Afonso)

Post, since he was an officer who served in Pontinha. Then, Commander Vítor Crespo joined him, representing the Navy and who was in contact with Lieutenant Captain Almada Contreiras, the latter at the Navy Communications Centre, located in the basement of the Navy Ministry.[62]

It was at 22:55 pm on *Rádio Clube Português* (RCP) when the voice of João Paulo Dinis gave the first signal for the revolution: Paulo de Carvalho with the Eurofestival of 74 song *E Depois do Adeus*.[63] As we have seen before, the song had won the RTP song festival in Portugal that year and would not arouse suspicion for playing on the radio at that hour.

In Vendas Novas, at the *Escola Prática de Artilharia*, the commander and the second-in-command were arrested, the radio station was occupied and the entrance to the barracks was controlled; then a general formation was organised with the presence of the military who decided to participate in the revolt.[64] In the EPI's Mafra barracks, the captains and subalterns were outside the unit and after hearing the signal they gathered to start the preparations for the mission; the captains and subalterns of the permanent staff of the EPAM went to the unit where they were armed and uniformed; in the *Caçadores* Battalion 5 (BC 5) in Lisbon, all adhered to the movement and were ordered to be armed and equipped. Equally prepared was the group of officers charged with storming the RCP to transform it into the MFA's outpost.

At 00:00 am the *Limite* programme started on *Rádio Renascença* with Paulo Coelho and Leite de Vasconcelos as speakers. It was in this radio station that the second signal was combined with a song by José Afonso. Leite Vasconcelos had been contacted on 24 April to play the song *Grândola, Vila Morena*, which would be received by the forces of the movement as the confirmation signal of the revolution. It was 00:20 am when Vasconcelos recited the first verse of the poem *Grândola, Vila Morena* and as soon as the song began to be sung there was great emotion at the Command Post in Pontinha.

A few minutes after the signal, there were military movements in several different units. In the EPAM officers' room, in Lumiar, the day officer and the officer on call were arrested and the MFA military took over the barracks. In Vendas Novas, at the EPA, a force of 180 men was organised and moved by several Berliet GBC trucks used to tow six 88mm cannons in the direction of Almada to take up position on top of the hill where the monument to Christ the King is located. From this position they completely dominated the Tagus River estuary and could also hit targets in Lisbon. North of the capital, in the detachment of the Serra da Carregueira firing range (CTSC), military personnel left in the direction of the capital to defend the Emissora Nacional studios. Even further north, in Mafra, military personnel were also preparing to leave in the direction of Lisbon to take over the airport. In Santa Margarida, one of the main Army bases, some military also begin to arm themselves to carry out the missions foreseen in the operational order.[65]

At 01:30 am, in Santarém, at the Cavalry Practical School (EPC), the order was given to wake up all personnel present. Being a cavalry unit, it had an important role in operations, as it could mobilise armoured vehicles and even some tanks. However, the EPC officers had already decided to leave the six M47 tanks they had at their disposal in Santarém, given the difficulty of travelling to Lisbon, and to focus on wheeled armoured vehicles. In the days

A Panhard EBR 75 armoured vehicle (right) on 25 April in downtown Lisbon. These armoured vehicles from Santarém were equipped with a 75mm cannon. A Panhard AML can also be seen in the centre of the picture. (Miranda Castela collection/Archive of the Assembly of the Republic)

preceding the uprising, they discreetly prepared a series of vehicles that would form the main force of the MFA in the Lisbon area.⁶⁶ In the early hours of the decisive night, Captain Salgueiro Maia and other EPC officers gathered the recruits who were attending military instruction in Santarém. To convince the recruits, Maia began his speech as follows:

> Gentlemen, as you all know, there are various forms of state. The socialist states, the capitalist states, and the state we are in. Now, in this solemn night, we are going to end this state. So, anyone who wants to come with me, we go to Lisbon, and we finish it. If you volunteer, go outside, and form up. If you do not want to go, stay here!

To the surprise of those present, the young troops joined enthusiastically and in large numbers.⁶⁷ However, of the approximately 500 soldiers in the barracks only 240 could participate, the rest would stay in Santarém to protect the installations and the sensitive points of the city. Thus, the EPC column, commanded by Salgueiro Maia, had more than 240 men, divided into two main groups. The first commanded by Captain Tavares de Almeida had 176 men in 12 troop transport vehicles. The second was a reconnaissance group commanded by Lieutenant Rui Santos Silva and had 56 men in 10 armoured vehicles (three Panhard EBR 75s, two Panhard AMLs and two Chaimites, and a Panhard ETT, a Humber, and a GMC Fox).⁶⁸ Of these vehicles, only the Panhard EBRs had significant firepower, as they were each equipped with a 75mm cannon.⁶⁹ Leading the column was a white Ford Escort with three non-uniformed officers to monitor the column's route and report any suspicious movement or obstacles in the way.⁷⁰ Salgueiro Maia later recounted that the police in Santarém would have noticed the vehicles leaving but must have thought they were leaving for a night exercise.⁷¹

At that time, the first difficulties also arose in Cascais, when the MFA officers were unable to take control of the CIAAC (*Centro de Instrução de Artilharia Antiaérea e de Costa*, Anti-aircraft and Coast Artillery Training Centre). Suspecting that something was going to happen that night, Major Pereira Rodrigues closed the gates of

Lisbon airport was an important point to occupy in Otelo's operations plan. The task was the responsibility of the military forces of Mafra, which moved towards the airport in the early morning of 25 April. (José Matos collection)

The *Rádio Clube Português* (RCP) had its broadcast centre in Porto Alto, 40km north of Lisbon. This centre was protected by troops from Santa Margarida so that the regime could not cut the broadcast. (RCP collection)

the unit and did not allow the young officers who were going to take over the CIAAC to enter, thus making it impossible for them to do so.⁷² There were also difficulties at the 3rd Cavalry Regiment in Estremoz, where the MFA men found it difficult to mobilise the necessary officers to march on Lisbon, especially the commander. After some hesitation, the unit commander eventually joined the movement in the middle of the night, which allowed him to organise a group with armoured vehicles and head towards Lisbon.⁷³

At 01:30 am at EPAM, the military who did not follow the coup were arrested in the library, while the rest prepared the forces to leave.⁷⁴ This force was commanded by Captain Teófilo Bento of the MFA, who organised a small military column with three vehicles leaving towards the television studios at 02:45 am.

At RI 14 in Viseu, the five MFA captains entered the barracks at 01:00 am and called all the officers to a meeting where they explained

Captain José Santos Coelho, Army engineer. It was this captain who proposed the taking of RCP and who did all the preparatory study for the assault. He had visited the radio studios previously and was also responsible for getting the weapons for the operation. It was also Santos Coelho who delivered the first communiqué of the MFA to the journalist Joaquim Furtado so that he could read it. (Carlos Coelho da Silva collection)

Joaquim Furtado was the journalist on duty who, at dawn on 25 April, read the first communiqué of the MFA on the RCP. (Carlos Coelho da Silva collection)

On 25 April, Luis Filipe Costa headed the RCP newsroom and was the voice that in the morning replaced Joaquim Furtado in the reading of the MFA communiqués. (Rui Pacheco collection)

Captain Santos Coelho was responsible for transmitting the MFA communiqués to the journalist on duty at the RCP. (Rui Pacheco collection)

the situation. They then woke up the soldiers who were sleeping in the barracks and prepared a company to head to Figueira da Foz to join Heavy Artillery Regiment 3 (RAP 3).[75]

In Mafra, the combat groups (around 280 men) were organised and went out at dawn to take over Portela airport. In BC 5, the personnel were lifted quietly so as not to arouse suspicion among the guards of the prison next to this barracks. Two of the battalion's companies would leave at 03:05 am: one to take care of the headquarters of the Lisbon Military Region and the other to protect the studios of *Rádio Clube Português*.[76]

It was just after 2:00 am when military personnel quartered in the Serra da Carregueira firing range, northwest of Lisbon, took to the streets in two heavy vehicles and a jeep and headed for the capital to seize the national broadcaster. Leading this 47-man force were captains Frederico Morais and Oliveira Pimentel, who arrived at the national radio station, located in Rua do Quelhas, at 03:00 am. Some police officers were guarding the station but were quickly persuaded to surrender by the men from Carregueira.[77] Meanwhile, at 02:45 am, a column of 100 men left EPAM in Lumiar and headed towards the studios of Portuguese television, which they stormed at 03:00 am, with practically no resistance, except for a policeman who was at the entrance of RTP, but who was disarmed.[78]

Shortly after that time, there were movements in the north of the country with a group of special forces commandos leaving Lamego towards Porto led by Captain Delgado Fonseca. This time, officers from Lamego, adherents of the MFA, took over the CIOE and detained the commander, Lieutenant Colonel José Sacramento Marques, who after some hesitation joined the coup. It was 03:00 am when the special forces group reinforced with heavy weapons elements equipped with mortars and several bazookas left Lamego for Porto.[79] Meanwhile, in the northern city, a military force from

Major Silva Pais, director of PIDE/DGS. In the early hours of 25 April, the head of the political police did not know that the revolution was in the streets and advised the Minister of Defence to sleep soundly. (PIDE/DGS)

Captain Costa Martins of the Air Force. On the night of the revolution, he was involved in the takeover of the Lisbon airport. (Carlos Coelho da Silva collection)

CICA 1 commanded by Lieutenant Colonel Carlos Azeredo, went to occupy the Headquarters of the Northern Military Region at 04:00 am, preventing any reaction against the movement's forces. It is interesting to note that at 04:30 am, the Army Minister, General Andrade e Silva, still made a phone call to the Northern HQ in Oporto to request that the Cavalry Regiment 6 (with headquarters in the city), march immediately to Lisbon in support of the government, but he soon realised that the HQ was held by the MFA and that he could not count on Cavalry Regiment 6.[80]

Meanwhile, in the capital, the *Rádio Clube* was surrounded at 03:15 am in the morning by a force from BC 5, commanded by Major José Cardoso Fontão. The group controlled access to the building, while inside a group of MFA officers took over the radio without much resistance from the staff on duty. This small group of officers consisted of three majors and five captains, who quickly occupied the radio studios in order to control the broadcast. Once the station was occupied, Captain Jose Santos Coelho called the Pontinha Command Post and informed them of the takeover at 03:20 am. Joaquim Furtado, the journalist on duty that dawn until late in the morning, read the first MFA communiqués to the population as provided by Santos Coelho.[81] Furtado was then replaced by Luis Filipe Costa, who was the editor-in-chief of RCP. Two voices pronouncing that unforgettable phrase that started every communiqué: 'Here is the command post of the Armed Forces Movement'.

In order to ensure the transmission, a combat group (CCAÇ. 4241/73) coming from Santa Margarida, commanded by Captain Luís Pessoa, took up position near the antennas of the RCP broadcasting centre in Porto Alto. This centre was located 40km north of Lisbon and ensured the transmission of the radio signal to the whole area of the Portuguese capital and their protection was extremely important.[82]

Part of the force that had left BC 5 would also occupy the headquarters of the Lisbon Military Region (*Região Militar de Lisboa*, RML). This second force of BC 5 was commanded by Captain Bicho Beatriz of the MFA that assaulted the headquarters of the RML, which was thus without its command centre.[83]

At 03:16 am, Army Minister, Andrade e Silva, was still in his office working and received a call from Defence Minister, Silva Cunha, who was also not sleeping. The two exchanged views on Andrade e Silva's visit to three barracks in the south of the country early in the

Mafra in the early 1960s, where the *Escola Prática de Infantaria* (EPI) was located. On 25 April, the force responsible for taking over the capital's airport departed from EPI. (Luís Correia de Sá Collection)

EPI forces from Mafra after taking over the capital's airport. (Flama archive)

Marcello Caetano's house in the Alvalade neighbourhood. It was from here that the head of government left for Carmo at the dawn of 25 April. (Miranda Castela collection/Archive of the Assembly of the Republic)

morning. As their phones were tapped, the conversation was heard at the Command Post in Pontinha. The Army Minister told Cunha that he was interested in going to Beja to attend a transmission of command and inspect the public order company. 'The commander there was a close friend of the man with the monocle [Spínola], whom he telephones often, so I had him mobilised for Overseas and placed another trustworthy person there, who takes office today,' Andrade e Silva said. Cunha asked him how the situation in the country was and Silva answered that 'the situation is unchanged and perfectly under control. I ask you not to worry, because everything is quiet and there is no problem anywhere in the country.' Cunha then wished him a good journey and said he was going home to sleep soundly.[84] This was one of the most emblematic moments of the state of government disinformation. With the revolution underway, the two ministers responsible for the military sector knew nothing of what was happening.

Silva Cunha would recall years later that between 16 March and 25 April 'there was a complete lack of information about what was being prepared.' The former minister also remembered the famous phone call on the night of 24–25 April. According to Silva Cunha it was Andrade e Silva who phoned him to tell that in the following morning he would be leaving Lisbon to visit some military units south of the Tagus River. In Silva Cunha's words, Andrade e Silva was 'unconcerned.' Later that night, Silva Cunha received a telephone call from the director of PIDE/DGS, Major Silva Pais, who told him the same thing: 'You can sleep soundly, Mr. Minister.' Silva Pais' phone call showed the state of ignorance in which the political police were that night.[85] Shortly afterwards, around 04:00 am, the minister received the bad news: 'the General Commander of the Public Security Police [PSP], General Tritão de Carvalhais, telephoned me, informing me that an armoured column from the Cavalry Practical School was advancing on Lisbon, having already passed Loures, and that a crowd of civilians and some military forces surrounded the Headquarters of the Military Government in Lisbon!'[86]

After the alert from the PSP commander, Silva Cunha warned the ministers of the Army and Navy, the Under-Secretary of State for the Army and CEMFGA. They all converged on the Ministry of the Army to confront the revolution, which was already in the streets. The Under-Secretary of State for the Army, Viana de Lemos, confirmed that he had been warned by the Minister of Defence and that, while still at home, he had received a phone call from Colonel Sousa Guerra, of the PSP, 'that forces from the Battalion of Hunters 5 (BC 5) were assaulting the headquarters of the Lisbon Military Region.'[87] Following the events, he phoned his brother-in-law – Romeiras Júnior – and they agreed that they would proceed to the Army Ministry in his private car, although, unknowingly, Romeiras Júnior was under surveillance by a group of MFA officers who nevertheless let him escape on the streets of Lisbon.[88]

At 04:26 am, Joaquim Furtado read the first communiqué of the MFA into the microphones of RCP appealing to the residents of Lisbon to stay in their homes and that the militarised forces avoid any confrontation with the Armed Forces. A second statement went out at 04:45 am, again appealing to the militarised and police

Rebel troops in Terreiro do Paço. This central area of Lisbon, near the Tagus River, was where the most important ministries were located. (Miranda Castela collection/Archive of the Assembly of the Republic)

An overall view of Lisbon, showing the Terreiro do Paço (centre) and the waterfront. The troops from Santarém quickly dominated this area, which came under MFA control. (Camera Press)

forces to stay in their barracks to avoid confrontations with the MFA forces.[89] At this time the airport had already been taken over by the forces that had come from the Infantry Practical School from Mafra. These forces were commanded by Captain Rui Rodrigues and easily occupied the airport facilities, where Captain Costa Martins from the Air Force was already waiting as if he were a normal passenger. Rui Rodrigues had become lost on his way to the airport with the military force from Mafra, which caused a delay in taking this objective. It was then up to Costa Martins to take over the control tower and interdict the Portuguese airspace.[90]

Marcello Caetano was warned of the military movements at around 05:00 am, by Major Silva Pais, who in turn warned the head of the government who was at home.[91] The director of PIDE/DGS told him that the revolution was in the streets, that the situation was serious and that he was trying to assess the true extent of the movement. Marcello immediately contacted Silva Cunha, who was at the Army Ministry and confirmed the information received. Silva Pais called Marcello back and advised him to leave home immediately and take refuge in the Carmo barracks, where the GNR General Command was based. However, the phone call was overheard at the MFA Command Post in Pontinha, and Otelo found out where the President of the Council was going. Marcello called his military adjutant, Commander Coutinho Lanhoso, and they prepared to go to Carmo.[92] Two PIDE/DGS agents, one of them being the driver of the car,[93] picked them up at home in the Alvalade neighbourhood.

On the way they came across troops that were near Terreiro do Paço, which Marcello thought were government forces, but were in fact rebels, probably troops from Santarém who had arrived at Terreiro do Paço just before 06:00 am. In fact, at that time, Salgueiro Maia had isolated the entire area, where several ministries were located, and the police forces that were already on the scene had begun to obey the orders of the young captain.[94]

At 06:15 am, Salgueiro Maia saw a squadron of Panhard AML and Chaimite vehicles arrive at Terreiro do Paço from Cavalry Regiment 7, commanded by a militia ensign, Luís David e Silva. The ensign stopped his vehicle next to Salgueiro Maia, who recognised him and asked what he was doing there. The latter told him that he had come by order of the government to defend the ministries. Maia replied that there was no longer a government, that the

MFA troops in front of the Army Ministry in Terreiro do Paço. This ministry was surrounded by Salgueiro Maia's troops, forcing the members of the government inside to flee through a hole in the wall. (Miranda Castela collection/Archive of the Assembly of the Republic)

ministers were stuck in the ministries and that the best thing was for him to join the movement, which he immediately did.⁹⁵ Salgueiro Maia then went to the Army Ministry to see who was there and found that the aspirant who commanded the Military Police (MP) platoon guarding the ministry had been his trainee. He persuaded him to switch to the side of the movement and thus took full control of the ministry, although he could not get into the building. The door to the ministry was still locked and the captain from Santarém hesitated to break it down. Sanches Osório, who was in Pontinha, recalled that a more senior officer, Lieutenant Colonel Correia de Campos, had to be sent to Terreiro do Paço to take control of the situation.⁹⁶

Initially, the ministers inside the building thought that Salgueiro Maia's troops were protecting the ministry and Silva Cunha sent a brigadier to Salgueiro Maia to thank him for the efficiency with which he had occupied positions in Terreiro do Paço. When Maia told him that the ministers were being held on the orders of the MFA, the leaders realised that the forces they could see through the window were in fact the insurgents.⁹⁷ Realising that they were surrounded, they tried to leave the ministry building and looked for an old communication door with the Ministry of the Navy, which was installed in the adjacent building. They discovered that the door had been covered with bricks, but they ordered the few soldiers of the MP who had remained inside the building to open a hole in the wall that separated the Ministry of the Army from the Ministry of the Navy. This is how the ministers of Defence, Silva Cunha; of the Army, Andrade e Silva; of the Interior, Moreira Baptista; of the Navy, Pereira Crespo; the CEMFGA, Joaquim da Luz Cunha; his brother, Edmundo da Luz Cunha, military governor of Lisbon; the Under-Secretary of State of the Army, Viana de Lemos and Admiral Henrique Tenreiro all escaped.⁹⁸

After escaping they went to *Regimento de Lanceiros 2* (RL 2), headquarters of the Military Police and which was one of the few units in the capital that still sided with the government. Moreira Baptista and Tenreiro would then go to Carmo barracks, where Marcello Caetano was taking refuge. But while they were still at the ministry, the military rulers gave the first orders for the Cavalry Regiment 7 forces to go into action. It was in this context that the first squadron of Cavalry Regiment 7 vehicles, with around 150 men, commanded by David e Silva appeared, which quickly switched to the side of the MFA, joining the rebel forces.⁹⁹ But it is not the only one. At 07:00 am a second squad equipped with Panhard EBR and ETT vehicles from the RC 7, commanded by Lieutenant Colonel Ferrand de Almeida arrived at Avenida da Ribeira das Naus near the Tagus River and close to the area where Salgueiro Maia was. The captain from Santarém went to meet him and told him there was no point in resisting and that he should surrender to the forces of the MFA, which Ferrand de Almeida ended up doing by passing his forces to the side of the rebels.¹⁰⁰ Ferrand de Almeida was arrested, and, in the evening, he was taken to the MFA operations centre in Pontinha. But the tensest moments of the morning were still to come. The first was with a Navy frigate that was involved that day in NATO's Standing Naval Force Atlantic (STANAVFORLANT) together with other NATO ships. The Portuguese frigate *Almirante Gago Coutinho* (F473) was about to leave Lisbon that morning, bound for Italy, to take part in a naval exercise, when the revolution happened. The ship, which was sailing on the Tagus, received orders from the Navy General Staff to abandon the NATO naval force and head for Terreiro do Paço. The order had come from the Minister of Defence himself, Silva Cunha, already installed in *Lanceiros 2*, who gave orders to the Chief of the Navy Staff, Admiral Ferreira da

A Panhard AML in the Terreiro do Paço area, next to the Tagus River. In the distance can be seen the silhouette of the frigate *Gago Coutinho* (F473), which was ordered to fire on Salgueiro Maia's forces. (Flama archive)

In Arsenal Street in downtown Lisbon, Salgueiro Maia's forces are confronted by two M47 tanks at the tensest moment of the revolution. (Flama archive)

Almeida, for the frigate to fire some warning shots on the rebellious forces that were in Terreiro do Paço.¹⁰¹ The order was received by the commander of the ship, António Seixas Louça, but he refused to fire, claiming that there were too many people in Terreiro do Paço, but he gave orders to the chief of the artillery service to fire a few shots in the air, an order that was not obeyed by the ship's crew. The frigate

A tense confrontation between M47s and Panhard EBRs on Arsenal Street in Lisbon. The tank crews did not obey orders to fire on rebel forces. (Miranda Castela collection/Archive of the Assembly of the Republic)

An M47 Patton in downtown Lisbon on Rua Augusta. This was one of the main battle tanks that went over to the rebel troops. (Rui Ochoa collection)

Arsenal Street and the other two advanced through Ribeira das Naus Avenue. In Arsenal it was Colonel Romeiras Júnior who commanded the two tanks, and in Ribeira das Naus it was Lieutenant Fernando Sottomayor accompanied by Major Pato Anselmo. Some troops followed behind. There were moments of great tension, when Salgueiro Maia tried to talk to Brigadier Junqueira dos Reis, demanding his surrender. The latter was obviously not willing to do so and ordered, more than once, the tanks to fire on Salgueiro Maia's forces, though the order was not obeyed by the men manning the battle tanks. Junqueira dos Reis was powerless before the men he commanded, who refuse to obey. Meanwhile, the Cavalry Regiment 7 forces that were in Ribeira das Naus switched to Captain Maia's side.[104] Major Pato Anselmo, who was in that street, surrendered and the two tanks that he had under his command went over to the side of the rebels. It was one of the decisive moments of the revolution. Some of the most powerful ground forces that the government had in its favour stopped defending the regime. From this point onwards, the ruling power could do little to confront the MFA forces.

Salgueiro Maia now had at his disposal the most powerful ground force in the city and completely controlled the area of Terreiro do Paço, where the ministries were located. The area was closed to the population trying to get to theire places of employment. 'I have to go to work and you have to let me through!' protested a cleaning woman from the post office in Terreiro do Paço. 'Oh! Go home, madam, today is a holiday. And next year too' replied Salgueiro Maia.[105]

Much further north, in Porto, the MFA troops had already secured control of the city but were experiencing major difficulties in communications. Technicians loyal to the regime had cut the telephone connections and sabotaged the Radio Club broadcast, which was not transmitting what was happening in the rest of the country. Thus, during the morning, the population of Porto knew nothing of what was happening in Lisbon.[106]

At the end of the morning, the captain from Santarém, received orders from Otelo to head for the barracks of Carmo, where Marcello Caetano was hiding.[107] Thus, at 11:30 am, the revolutionary forces

ended up having a passive attitude towards Salgueiro Maia's forces, who obviously feared that the ship might fire on the movement's forces.[102] However, in case of conflict, the artillery at Cristo-Rei, on the other side of the Tagus River, could fire on the frigate, and the Command Post also had two F-86 fighters available at the Monte Real base, which could take off at any time of the day.[103]

The second moment was with the last armoured forces of Cavalry Regiment 7, commanded by the second-in-command of the Lisbon Military Region, Brigadier Junqueira dos Reis, who brought with him four M47 Patton tanks that represented a serious threat to Salgueiro Maia's forces, which were mainly equipped with lightly armoured vehicles. Confronting a main battle tank was something the young captain wanted to avoid at all costs. But he was confronted by the squadron commanded by Junqueira dos Reis, around 10:00 am, in two streets near Terreiro Paço. Two M47s entered through

The population in the streets of Lisbon applauded the soldiers enthusiastically. (Miranda Castela collection/Archive of the Assembly of the Republic)

Troops and people around the quarter of "Largo do Carmo" where former Prime Minister Marcello Caetano and some of the members of his cabinet surrendered to the military movement. (Europa Press)

that were concentrated in Terreiro do Paço were given new missions and the young captain set off in the direction of the GNR barracks. On the way, he also met a force from the Regiment of Infantry 1 (RI1) from Amadora, commanded by Captain Fernandes, who had been sent by the government, but who also joined the movement.[108] The progress through the city streets was slow, with the troops being applauded by the people in the streets of downtown Lisbon, who shouted various slogans: 'Vitória! Vitória!' and 'Abaixo o fascismo (down with fascism).' Salgueiro Maia himself recognised 'that when our forces marched towards Carmo they heard the biggest apotheosis that the Armed Forces must have had for many years. With an encouragement like that I was sure that none of my soldiers had any doubts about what they were doing.'[109]

The forces from Santarém, reinforced by RI 1, arrived at Largo do Carmo shortly after noon and set up a siege around the barracks, blocking the main accesses. Meanwhile, Junqueira dos Reis, with the rest of the Cavalry Regiment 7 forces, a company from RI 1, a squad from the GNR that was under the order of the Military Government of Lisbon, and some military police, tried to surround Salgueiro Maia's forces, but was unsuccessful. Otelo ordered the Cavalry Regiment 3 forces that were arriving in Lisbon from Estremoz to go to Carmo to support the troops from Santarém.[110] With the arrival of the forces from Estremoz, the contingent loyal to the regime eventually demobilised without taking any initiative.[111]

In Carmo barracks, besides Marcello Caetano, the Minister of the Interior, Moreira Baptista and the Minister of Foreign Affairs, Rui Patrício, were also present. The command of the government forces was in *Lanceiros 2* with Silva Cunha and Andrade e Silva. In the command office, the two ministers desperately tried to mobilise forces to counter the military uprising but could do nothing. The few forces that showed any loyalty to the regime demobilised or were unable to intervene.

During the day, PIDE/DGS still tried to remove the head of the government from Carmo. Silva Pais called Marcello and a group of the political police was sent in two cars to extract the President of the Council through the back of the barracks, but he refused to leave, arguing that he was only leaving through the door he had entered.[112] At *Lanceiros 2*, Silva Cunha still tried to mobilise a helicopter to remove Marcello Caetano from Carmo, but the place was unsuitable for the helicopter to land.[113] Meanwhile, elsewhere in *Lanceiros 2*, some officers protested against the presence of the ministers in the barracks, and, on the advice of the unit commander, the members of the government requested a helicopter that took them to Monsanto, to the headquarters of the 1st Air Region Command, while the remaining individuals with them left the barracks by car. In Monsanto, they were received by Air Force General Rui Tavares Monteiro and again established contact with Marcello Caetano, who was already in talks with General Spínola to hand over power.[114] The head of government had finally realised that it was useless to resist and that he had to hand over power to someone with prestige and authority.

So That Power Does Not Fall Onto the Street

In mid-afternoon, Salgueiro Maia began to issue a series of ultimatums from outside the barracks for the surrender of the GNR and the members of the government who were inside. Faced with no response, the young captain ordered his soldiers to fire on the front of the building. Even after the shooting, the GNR did not surrender. At this point, Major Velasco of the GNR, who was involved in the movement, appeared outside, and tried to calm the situation. Salgueiro Maia demanded his surrender, and the major went back inside to tell the GNR commander-general about it.[115] The impasse continued, and the captain of Santarém was willing to do anything to obtain the surrender of the occupants of the GNR headquarters. During the tensest moments of the afternoon, he even ordered aspirant José Manuel Sampaio, who was commanding the

Salgueiro Maia with a loudspeaker in hand addresses the crowd at Largo do Carmo in front of the Republican Guard headquarters. (AP)

Salgueiro Maia with Major Velasco of the GNR, in Largo do Carmo, on the afternoon of 25 April. (Miranda Castela collection/Archive of the Assembly of the Republic)

Spínola's car at the moment he arrived in Carmo. It was with great difficulty that the car passed through the crowd that received the general in great euphoria. (Flama archive)

Panhard EBR closest to the barracks gate, to move into position to open fire. However, Sampaio realised that he could cause casualties among the crowd surrounding the barracks if he fired at the gate and decided to pretend not to hear the captain's order, thus avoiding a tragedy.[116]

Meanwhile, two men from the Secretary of State for Information and Tourism, Pedro Feytor Pinto and Nuno Távora, had arrived at Carmo to take a written message from Marcello Caetano to General Spínola.[117] In the message, the head of the government said that he did not want power to fall onto the street and the blood of the Portuguese to be shed in vain, and that he thought Spínola was the person in the best condition to assume power.[118] This position had been taken by Marcello after hearing Rui Patrício, who was with him in the GNR headquarters, and Pedro Pinto, Secretary of State for Information and Tourism, who had spoken on the phone with the President of the Council. It is interesting to note that Spínola emerged as a protagonist on the day of the revolution largely due to Pedro Pinto's actions. It was this member of the government who, given the gravity of the situation, tried to contact Spínola and mediate a solution between the general and the head of the government. He was the one who telephoned Spínola and wrote him a letter urging the general to take a position so that the troops would have a chief.[119] Pedro Pinto had good relations with Spínola and knew that the general had influence with the captains, and when he realised that the rebels had given the government a deadline to surrender, he tried to convince Spínola to intervene in the events. But the general hesitated and told Pedro Pinto that he was not the one who made the revolution, nor was he at the head of the movement, and that he could only do something if he was asked to do so by the President of the Republic, by Marcello Caetano or by the rebels, through people duly mandated.[120] In view of this reply, Pedro Pinto wrote a message to be taken to Marcello Caetano by two men in his trust – Nuno Távora and Feytor Pinto – where one could read that Spínola was available to assume power and take charge of the situation, if so requested by the President of the Council.[121] After receiving the two emissaries at the Carmo barracks, Caetano realised that there was a way out and decided to contact Spínola. It was at this point that Rui Patrício drafted a message, which was then written up by Coutinho Lanhoso, Marcello's military advisor, to be hand delivered to the general's home.[122] Feytor Pinto and Távora were then ordered to go to Spínola's house with the message to convey Marcello's wishes. The general received the two emissaries with suspicion and did not recognise Marcello's handwriting in the letter (the message had actually been handwritten by Coutinho Lanhoso). According to a photocopy of a handwritten document written that day in Carmo's barracks, the message had the following content: 'I consider it absolutely indispensable that someone with responsibilities takes care of the situation, otherwise the power will fall onto the street. I am at General Spínola's disposal in Carmo barracks.' The last part of this manuscript had been erased and it is only possible to read: 'For the rest, I will only give myself up to him.' It is presumed this sentence is Marcello's own handwriting or that of someone to whom he dictated it, given the high level of tension he was experiencing.[123]

Only after receiving a phone call from Marcello Caetano did Spínola become convinced that the message was true: 'General, I have to acknowledge that I am defeated. [...] If the government has to capitulate, let it be before someone who can take responsibility for public order and reassure the country' Marcello Caetano told Spínola on the phone. The general still argued that he was not involved in the conspiracy, but Marcello insisted that he should be the one to take power. However, before taking any action, Spínola contacted Otelo in Pontinha to ask for permission to go to Carmo to receive power from the hands of the head of the government, who wanted to surrender.[124] Otelo gave him the green light and the general then went to Carmo to deal with the capitulation.[125] Meanwhile, Salgueiro Maia had already entered the building and demanded Marcello's surrender. After several tense moments, Maia decided to enter and speak personally with the President of the Council.[126] The captain reported the meeting face to face with Caetano:

> They led me to Marcello Caetano's presence; but for that I passed through an antechamber, where Moreira Baptista and Rui Patrício were, the latter crying like a child, the former looking into infinity. Marcello was pale, beard unshaven, tie loosened, but dignified. I saluted him and told him I wanted an immediate and formal surrender. He told me he had already surrendered to General Spínola, by telephone, and was only awaiting his arrival to transfer power to him, so that power would not fall onto the street.[127]

Caetano must have been perplexed to find that the commander of the forces surrounding the building was a mere captain. He still tried to find out who was behind the revolution, but Salgueiro Maia said little about the leaders of the revolution. The ruler had already understood that he could only hand over power to someone with the authority and prestige to take over the country's destiny and that someone could only be General Spínola. However, the captain from Santarém knew nothing of these contacts, but quickly realised that Caetano had already negotiated the surrender.

It was almost 06:00 pm when General Spínola entered Carmo barracks, with the population cheering enthusiastically at his arrival.

Lieutenant Colonel Ferreira da Cunha who arranged for Costa Gomes to go to the military hospital on the day of the revolution so as not to arouse suspicion if the coup failed. (Revista do Povo collection)

Costa Gomes and his wife in 1974. On the day of the revolution, they were both in the military hospital to cover up any involvement with the coup attempt if it failed. (AP)

It is with great difficulty that Spínola's car crossed the crowd. Inside, the general was led by the commander of the GNR, General Adriano Pires, to Caetano's office. After a brief conversation, the former ruler left the fate of the country in Spínola's hands. After Marcello's surrender, Spínola arranged with Salgueiro Maia for the head of government and the ministers to be taken to Pontinha. It was the captain of Santarém who provided a Chaimite vehicle to take the former members of the government to the MFA Command Post. Marcello's surrender was communicated to Silva Pais by the head of the PIDE/DGS that had taken the President of the Council to Carmo, Diogo de Albuquerque: 'It's over, our President is going to give himself up to General Spínola.' At the political police headquarters,

The Chaimite named *Bula* enters GNR headquarters to remove Marcello Caetano and two other ministers, Rui Patrício and Moreira Baptista. They were transported to the MFA Command Post at the Pontinha. (Miranda Castela collection/Archive of the Assembly of the Republic)

inspector Pereira de Carvalho ordered the staff to burn compromising documents.[128]

Meanwhile, Spínola tried to find out where Costa Gomes was, who had been out of contact all day. Carlos de Morais told him that Costa Gomes had spent the day at the military hospital together with his wife, who had gone to the hospital for a series of routine examinations. It was also Carlos de Morais who called the military hospital from the Carmo barracks and asked Spínola to speak with Costa Gomes.[129] Costa Gomes' trip to the hospital with his wife on the day of the revolution had been a ploy not to commit himself to the military coup. If, by any chance, the coup had failed, the general could say he knew nothing about it. At least one week before 25 April, Costa Gomes went to the military hospital on the pretext that his wife, Estela, had to undergo examination. The ex-CEMGFA took a suitcase with all the documents he needed, including his passport, in case he had to leave the country. There he stayed with his wife and received visitors, such as his former chief of staff, Lieutenant Colonel Ferreira da Cunha, who brought him messages from the MFA. In the event of the coup failing, the police or the PIDE/DGS could arrest him if he was at home, in the centre of Lisbon, whereas in the military hospital he was more protected, and could not be arrested so easily. So that there would be no suspicion as to his strategy, Ferreira da Cunha brought his wife during the visits, who 'went to visit her friend' at the hospital, according to his son, Luís Campos e Cunha. This attitude would be understandable given that on 16 March the PIDE had followed Ferreira da Cunha on a visit he made to the home of the ex-CEMGFA.[130]

At 07:30 pm, the Chaimite reversed through the main gate of the GNR barracks, with Marcello Caetano and the two former ministers, Rui Patrício and Moreira Baptista entering.[131] The armoured vehicle slowly made its way through the angry crowd, who booed the former ministers, being escorted in front and in the rear by three Panhard AMLs.[132] Spínola accompanied the motorcade in a separate car, which would be stoned on the way, probably because some people thought it was carrying the PIDE/DGS.[133] The streets of Lisbon were full of people who never tired of shouting, 'Victory! Victory!' as the Chaimite headed towards the Command Post in Pontinha. The joy was contagious, and people everywhere celebrated the end of the long dictatorship. During the day, the daily newspapers had given the first news about the coup in extra editions. It was the first time that the news had come out without prior censorship.

This euphoria also reached Porto, where radio broadcasting had already been restored by mid-afternoon, allowing the city's inhabitants to know what was happening in Lisbon. At around 05:00 pm, many people gathered in downtown Porto, namely on the city's main thoroughfare, Avenida dos Aliados (Allies Avenue), excited by

Moments of tension on Porto's main thoroughfare, Avenue of the Allies, when police attacked the crowd on the afternoon of 25 April, causing several injuries. (Pereira de Sousa collection)

The people of Lisbon celebrate the end of the long dictatorship in a great explosion of joy. (José Sanchez Martinez collection)

One of Portugal's daily newspapers announce the military coup on its cover. It was the first time that newspapers were published without prior censorship. (A Capital)

Otelo Saraiva de Carvalho was the key man during the revolution. It was he who commanded the operations from Pontinha with the other MFA officers. (F. Gonçalves collection/AEI)

Time magazine in its 6 May edition highlighted Spínola on its cover. The general appeared as the natural leader of the Portuguese revolution. (TIME Magazine)

the news coming from the capital. Several hundred people gathered in the area to greet the military coup. At that time, the police commander in Porto, Colonel Santos Júnior, contacted MFA officers who were at CICA 1 (which functioned as an Alternative Command Post) and announced that he would disperse the crowd using force. The MFA officers forbade Santos Júnior to take any repressive action, but the police who were in the area intervened against the people on Avenida dos Aliados, dispersing the crowd with batons. Some young people reacted and started throwing stones at the police force, who were forced to seek refuge. By then, a group of MFA soldiers were in a nearby street, Rua de Ceuta, re-established telephone communications that had been cut off and, seeing the attitude of the police, they intervened in favour of the civilians. But the clashes did not end there. The people started to walk up Avenida dos Aliados towards the Town Hall shouting slogans in favour of the revolution and were again attacked by the police who were near the Post Office Palace. This time, the agents draw their pistols and fired on the crowd, injuring several people.[134]

Meanwhile, the main leaders of the government forces in Lisbon were arrested in Monsanto, at the 1st Airborne Region Command, where they had gone after abandoning *Lanceiros 2*; a small force of the military from Mafra, who had taken over the airport, then went to Monsanto to arrest the Army and Navy Defence ministers and take them to the Command Post in Pontinha.[135] Unlike other individuals, Américo Thomaz took refuge in the Forte de Porto Salvo in Paço de Arcos, near Lisbon, but, in the evening, he returned to his private residence, staying overnight at home until he was taken at dawn to the military airport in Lisbon to go to the island of Madeira, where he would stay until a better solution was found.[136]

The day after the revolution, an anecdote circulated in the Portuguese capital about the difficulty the President of the Republic had in understanding what had happened to him on 25 April.[137] 'But what is this about a coup d'état?' he would ask, adding: 'And so I wasn't consulted?'

The main figures of the regime would spend the night in Pontinha. Marcello would spend much of the night talking to Silva Cunha, Moreira Baptista and Pereira Crespo about the future of the country and Overseas Territories.[138] The following morning, Caetano, Thomaz, Silva Cunha, and Moreira Baptista were taken to the airport and put on a plane to Madeira. From there, Marcello

Caetano would leave for exile in Brazil, never to return to Portugal. As for the remaining members of the government, some would go home and others to prison.[139]

On the night of 25 April, around 08:30 pm, Spínola arrived in Pontinha to greet the strategists of the revolution and arrange the formation of the National Salvation Junta (*Junta de Salvação Nacional*, JSN) that would temporarily rule the country. Upon arrival, he was received by Otelo, to whom he gave a strong hug, and then went to the operations room, where the remaining MFA members were waiting for him.[140] He praised the men of the MFA for the act of transcendental importance for the history of the country that they had carried out and that a different society could now be built in a new Portugal. 'The Homeland is grateful to you,' said Spínola.[141] Commenting on the situation later, Otelo admitted that nobody had the courage to tell Spínola that he was not the man chosen by the MFA to preside over the military junta, but Costa Gomes.[142]

Fialho Gouveia presents the members of the military junta on public TV. From left to right: Rosa Coutinho, Pinheiro de Azevedo, Costa Gomes, Spínola, Jaime Silvério Marques and Galvão de Melo. Only Diogo Neto, who was in Mozambique, was missing. Spínola leads. (Carlos Gil collection)

However, the truth was that António de Spínola emerged as the natural leader of the revolution, although for much of the day he hesitated to openly support the movement of captains, and only took on the leading role when Caetano asked him to go to Carmo to receive power. Furthermore, Costa Gomes also suggested that Spínola be the one to take the reins of the military junta, as he felt that Spínola had good relations with the political sectors and the press and would therefore be the right person to occupy the presidency of the military junta.[143]

Little by little, the elements of the military junta arrived in Pontinha, and several discussions took place around the MFA programme.[144] Obviously, Spínola tried to control the situation and officers such as Otelo felt overwhelmed. The discussion on the MFA's programme, of which Spínola had prior knowledge, continued. The general wanted to make some changes, which the MFA military did not accept.[145] Hours passed and in response to Spínola's insistence, the captains threatened to return the armoured forces to the streets if a consensus was not reached. The junta was presented to the country at dawn, when the announcer on *Radio Televisão Portuguesa*, Fialho Gouveia, presented one by one the military that would govern Portugal in the near future with Spínola at the head. The two most prominent figures at the table were obviously Spínola and Costa Gomes, with the latter assuming the position of CEMGFA.[146] The remaining five members of the military junta were officers from the Army, Air Force and Navy, which guaranteed the representativeness of the three branches in this new power structure.[147]

The Fall of PIDE/DGS

However, despite the change of regime, the PIDE/DGS still resisted that night. The political police would be the last institution of the dictatorship to fall. It would also be the only one to cause casualties when it fired twice on the people who were approaching the headquarters on the day of the revolution.[148] Had it not been for

MFA soldiers control the access road to the headquarters of the political police in Lisbon. The PIDE/DGS was the last institution of the Portuguese dictatorship to fall and the only one that caused casualties among the population. (Flama archive)

this desperate act, the Portuguese revolution would have taken place without bloodshed. The taking of the PIDE/DGS was not a priority in Otelo's plans, as the political police did not exactly pose a military threat to the movement's forces. However, when the agents' shots claimed victims in the crowd, the MFA was forced to act.

To put an end to the resistance, Spínola telephoned Silva Pais that night, reprimanding him for the events and demanding his surrender. The director then placed himself under the command of the new power.[149] Throughout the night Army forces (Cavalry Regiment 3 from Estremoz), later reinforced by Navy Marines, surrounded the area where the political police headquarters were located.[150] Little by little, some agents left during the night, being arrested, and searched by the troops outside.

On the morning of the 26th, shortly after 08:00 am, Spínola gave the first press conference of the military junta, in Pontinha, in

The three paintings with the images of Américo Thomaz, Marcello Caetano, and Salazar in the political police headquarters. (Miranda Castela collection/Archive of the Assembly of the Republic)

A room with files kept inside the PIDE/DGS headquarters is watched over by a Navy Marine. (Michel Puech collection)

which he clearly stated that the extinction of the DGS was planned, only with the exception of Overseas, as long as military operations required it.[151] Shortly after this press conference, the forces outside PIDE/DGS started preparing to enter the building. Contact had taken place already that morning between inspector Rogério Coelho Dias and the military who surrounded the building, in order for the political police to surrender.[152] It is known from the newspapers of the time that it was 09:30 am, when a Marine officer, Melo Saigão, approached the journalists and announced the surrender of PIDE/DGS.[153] A little later at 09:43 am, a group formed by officers and journalists, led by Lieutenant Captain Luís Costa Correia of the Navy, who was supervising the force of Marines, entered the headquarters of the political police.[154] A few minutes later, the military forces occupied the organisation's central building.[155] The officers of the besieging forces ordered the disarming of all the occupants inside the building and the Marines under the command of Costa Correia eventually occupied the organisation's headquarters. Contrary to what might be expected, the archives of the political police containing millions of files were found apparently intact.[156] Inside the rooms, a large quantity of weapons was also found. On the desks of some agents, they also found *Playboy* and *Penthouse* magazines, which were not sold in Portugal. The former agents were arrested and would be sent at the end of the day to Caxias prison, where political prisoners, victims of PIDE/DGS itself, were usually held.[157] In Silva Pais's office, three paintings with images of Américo Thomaz, Marcello Caetano and Salazar remained fixed on the wall. Orders were given to remove them, and Silva Pais was ready to do it, but the portrait of Salazar was more difficult to remove because it was higher and it is said that someone then went to get a ladder and it too was removed.[158] The end of the regime was consummated.

Soldiers celebrate the fall of the regime in Lisbon and the beginning of a new era in Portugal. (Miranda Castela collection/Archive of the Assembly of the Republic)

A glorified vision of Spínola in which the Portuguese people thank the general for 25 April. (José Matos collection)

Costa Gomes and Spínola were the two most prominent figures to emerge from the April revolution. Spínola would be the leader for a few months, but in late September 1974 he would be replaced by Costa Gomes. (Luís Gonçalves collection)

Marcello Caetano and Silva Cunha during their brief exile on the island of Madeira. (Madeira Museum of Photography)

The April revolution in Portugal, the great people's party. (Inácio Ludgero collection)

SOURCES AND BIBLIOGRAPHY

Archives
Archives du MAE
Archive of the Assembly of the Republic
General Directorate of Archives (DGARQ)
Historical Archive of the Presidency of the Republic (AHPR)
Historical Diplomatic Archive (AHD)
Marcelo Caetano Archive (AMC)
Military Historical Archive (AHM)
National Archive of Torre do Tombo (ANTT)
National Archives, Washington D.C.
National Defence Archive (ADN)
Overseas Historical Archive (AHU)
Presidency of the Republic Museum – António de Spínola Archive (MPR/AAS)

Documentaries
Furtado, Joaquim, *A Guerra*, RTP 2008, 42 episodes.
Pontes, Joana, *A Hora da Liberdade*, SIC 1999.

Press
Several newspapers and magazines were consulted in the research for this book:
A Capital
Diário de Notícias
Diário Popular
Expresso
Flama
Gazeta das Caldas
Jornal de Macau
L'Express Afrique
Le Figaro
Le Monde
Mais Alto
Manchete
Newsweek
O Dia
O Mundo Português
O Seculo Ilustrado
Publico
Rand Daily Mail
República
Sempre Fixe
Tal & Qual
The Daily Telegraph
The Sunday Telegraph
The Financial Times
Washington Star News

Bibliography
AAVV, *25 de Abril, Os 240 que prenderam Caetano, A coluna militar da EPC* (Lisbon: Special edition of the *Público* newspaper on the 25th anniversary of the 25th of April 1999).
AAVV, *O Pronunciamento Militar do 25 de Abril 1974*, V Conference of the Núcleo Impulsionador das Conferências da Cooperativa Militar (NICCM) (Lisbon: NICCM Edition, 2014)
Abreu, Paradela, *Do 25 de Abril ao 25 de Novembro: memória do tempo perdido* (Lisbon: Intervenção, 1983)
Abreu, Paradela de (Coord.), *Os Últimos Governadores do Império* (Lisbon: Edições Neptuno, 1994)
Almeida, Dinis, *Origens e evolução do Movimento de Capitães: subsídios para uma melhor compreensão,* 2nd edition (Lisbon: Ed.Sociais, 1977)
Almeida, Luís Pinheiro and Cabral, Rui, *25 de Abril, memórias* (Lisbon: Agência Lusa, special edition, 1994)
Amaral, Diogo Freitas do, *O Antigo Regime e a Revolução Memórias Políticas (1941-1975)* (Venda Nova: Edições Bertrand/Nomen, 1995)
Andrade, Nuno, *Para Além do Portão. A GNR e o Carmo na Revolução de Abril* (Lisbon: Guerra e Paz, 2007)
Antunes, José Freire, *Os Americanos e Portugal* Vol. I *Os anos de Richard Nixon 1969-1974* (Lisbon: Publicações Dom Quixote, 1986)
Antunes, José Freire, *Nixon e Caetano: Promessas e Abandono-1969-1974* (Lisbon: Difusão Cultural, 1992)
Arriaga, Kaúlza de, *Guerra e Política: Em nome da Verdade, Os Anos Decisivos,* 2nd edition (Lisbon: Edições Referendo, 1987)
Azeredo, Carlos de Azeredo, *Trabalhos e Dias de Um Soldado do Império* (Porto: Livraria Civilização Editora, 2004)
Baptista, Jacinto, *Caminhos para uma Revolução* (Amadora: Livraria Bertrand, 1975)
Barroso, José Manuel, *Segredos de Abril* (Lisbon: Editorial Notícias, 1995)
Bernardo, Manuel, *Marcello e Spínola: A Ruptura. As Forças Armadas e a Imprensa na Queda do Estado Novo, 1973-1974* (Lisbon: Edições Margem, 1999)
Bernardo, Manuel, *Equívocos e Realidades – Portugal 1974-1975*, Vol. I (Lisbon: Nova Arrancada, 1999)
Bernardo, Joaquim Manuel Correia, *Santarém. Uma cidade que faz História. 25 de Abril de 1974* (Santarém: Research Centre Professor Doutor Joaquim Veríssimo Serrão, 2015)
Brito, Carlos, *Álvaro Cunhal Sete fôlegos de um combatente* (Lisbon: Edições Nelson de Matos, 2010)
Caetano, Marcello, *Depoimento* (Rio de Janeiro: Distribuidora Record, 1974)
Caetano, Marcello, *O 25 de Abril e o Ultramar. Três entrevistas e alguns documentos* (Lisbon: Verbo, 1977)
Caio, Horácio, *Guinea 74 – Vigilância e Resposta* (Lisbon: 1974)
Câmara, Maria João da, *Sanches Osório. Memórias de uma Revolução* (Alfragide: Oficina do Livro, 2019)
Carvalho, Otelo Saraiva de, *Alvorada em Abril* (Lisbon: Bertrand, 1977)
Carvalho, Otelo Saraiva de, *O dia inicial. 25 de Abril. Hora a Hor* (Lisbon: Editora Objectiva, 2011)
Castanheira, José Pedro, "O encontro que veio demasiado tarde", *Expresso* Magazine no. 1117, March 26, 1994
Castanheira, José Pedro, "Conversações em Roma", *Expresso* Magazine no. 1226, April 27, 1996
Central Intelligence Bulletin, March 15, 1974, CIA-RDP-79T00975A026200001-8, CIA Records Search Tool (CREST), National Archives and Records Administration
Charais, Franco, *História Viva – 25 de Abril: Golpe Militar ou Revolução?* (Lisbon: Âncora Editora, 2013)
Chenel, Bernard [et al.], *Mirage III/5/50 en service à l'étranger* (Le Vigen: Lela Presse, 2014)

Coelho, Adelino de Matos, "Sobre o 16 de Março de 1974", *Gazeta das Caldas*, April 28, 2022

Contreiras, Carlos de Almada [et al.], *Operação Viragem Histórica: 25 Abril 1974*, 2nd Edition (Lisbon: Edições Colibri, 2018)

Costa Gomes, Francisco da, Manuel, Alexandre, *Sobre Portugal: Diálogos com Alexandre Manuel* (Lisbon: A Regra do Jogo, 1979)

Costeira, Arnaldo, *Eu Capitão de Abril me confesso* (Porto: Lello Editores, 1999)

Coutinho, Pereira, "Exército Português – Auto-Metralhadoras" (2nd part), *Revista da Cavalaria* no. 27, May/August 2012

Crespo, Manuel Pereira, *Porque Perdemos a Guerra* (Edições Abril, 1977)

Cruz, Manuel Braga da, Ramos, Rui (org.), *Marcello Caetano – Tempos de Transição* (Porto: Porto Editora, 2012)

Cruzeiro, Maria Manuela, *Costa Gomes: O último marechal* (Lisbon: Editorial Notícias, 1998)

Cruzeiro, Maria Manuela, *Melo Antunes, O sonhador pragmático*, 3rd edition (Lisbon: Editorial de Notícias, 2005)

Cruzeiro, Maria Manuela, *Vasco Lourenço do Interior da Revolução* (Lisbon: Âncora Editora, 2009)

Cunha, Silva, *O Ultramar, a Nação e o 25 de Abril* (Coimbra: Atlântida Editora, 1977)

Cunha, Silva, *Ainda o 25 de Abril* (Lisbon: Centro do Livro Brasileiro, 1984)

Cunha, Alfredo, Gomes, Adelino, *Os rapazes dos tanques* (Porto: Porto Editora, 2014)

Crespo, Manuel Pereira, *Porque Perdemos a Guerra* (Edições Abril, 1977)

Cruz, Manuel Braga da and Ramos, Rui, (Org.), *Marcelo Caetano: Tempos de Transição* (Porto: Porto Editora, 2012)

Frazão, António and Filipe, Maria do Céu Barata, *Arquivo Marcello Caetano,* Volumes I and II (Lisbon: Instituto dos Arquivos Nacionais/Torre do Tombo, 2005)

Golias, Jorge Sales, *A Descolonização da Guiné-Bissau e o Movimento dos Capitães,* 2nd edition (Lisbon: Edições Colibri, 2017)

Gomes, Bernardino and Sá, Tiago Moreira de, *Carlucci vs Kissinger – Os EUA e a Revolução Portuguesa* (Lisbon: Dom Quixote, 2008)

Hernandez, Humberto C. Trujillo, *El Grito del Baobab* (Habana: Editorial de Ciências Sociales, 2008)

Jardim, Jorge, *Moçambique – Terra Queimada* (Lisbon: Editorial Intervenção, 1976)

Júnior, J. Plácido, "25 de Abril: A história nunca contada dos três azarados da coluna de Salgueiro Maia", *Visão* magazine, May 1, 2021

Lã, João Rosa, *Do Outro Lado das Coisas – (In)Confidências Diplomáticas,* 3rd Edition (Santa Cruz: Book Builders/Letras Errantes, 2015)

Lauret, Pedro, *O Dia da Liberdade. 25 de Abril de 1974* (Vila do Conde: Verso da História, 2015)

Lemos, Mário Matos e, *O 25 de Abril – Uma síntese, uma perspetiva* (Lisbon: Editorial Notícias, 1986)

Lemos, Viana de, *Duas Crises, 1961 e 1974 – um olhar de um oficial do exército português,* 2nd edition (Lisbon: Edições Cosmos, 2009)

Loudon, Bruce, "Portuguese forces put on alert", *The Sunday Telegraph*, March 10, 1974

Loudon, Bruce, "Africa War Crisis Grips Portugal", *The Daily Telegraph*, March 11, 1974

Loudon, Bruce, "Portuguese Cabinet shake-up likely in bid to defuse army crisis", *The Financial Times*, March 13, 1974

Loudon, Bruce, "How the mighty pen split Portugal", *The Sunday Telegraph*, March 17, 1974

Magalhães, J. Calvet de, *O 25 de Abril e as Necessidades* (Lisbon: Estratégia – Revista de Estudos Internacionais, IEEI, 2004)

Maia, Matos, *Aqui Emissora da Liberdade: Rádio Clube Português 04.26 25 de Abril de 1974* (Lisbon: Edição Rádio Clube Português, 1975)

Maia, Salgueiro, *Capitão de Abril. Histórias da Guerra do Ultramar e do 25 de Abril* (Lisbon: Editorial News, 1997)

Manuel, Alexandre, Carapinha, Rogério, Neves, Dias (eds.), *PIDE: a história da repressão* (Fundão: Jornal do Fundão, 1974)

Marques, Silvino Silvério, *Portugal e Agora?* (Lisbon: Edições do Templo, 1978)

Marques, Silvino Silvério, *Marcello Caetano, Angola e o 25 de Abril – Uma Polémica com Veríssimo Serrão* (Mem Martins: Editorial Inquérito, 1995)

Matos, José, "A História Secreta dos Mirages Portugueses", *Mais Alto* magazine No. 400 (Nov/Dec 2012) and *Mais Alto* No. 401 (Jan/Feb 2013)

Matos, José, Barroso, Luís, *Nos Meandros da Guerra – O Estado Novo e a África do Sul na Defesa da Guiné* (Lisbon: Caleidoscópio, 2020)

Mello, Manuel José Homem de, *Meio Século de Observação* (Lisbon: Círculo de Leitores, 1996)

Monteiro, Pedro, *Berliet, Chaimite e UMM – Os Grandes Veículos Militares Nacionais* (Lisbon: Contra Corrente, 2018)

Monteiro, Fábio, *Esquecidos em Abril – Os Mortos da Revolução sem Sangue* (Lisbon: Livros Horizonte, 2019)

Moura, Paulo, *Otelo – O Revolucionário* (Lisbon: Publicações Dom Quixote, 2012)

Morais, Carlos Alexandre de, *António de Spínola – O Homem* (Lisbon: Editorial Estampa, 2007)

Múrias, Manuel Maria, *De Salazar a Costa Gomes* (Lisbon: Nova Arrancada, 1998)

Ockrent, Christine, Marenches, Count of, *No Segredo dos Deuses* (Lisbon: Edições Referendo, 1988)

Oliveira, Zélia Costa de, *Os 63 dias que abalaram o Estado Novo – Incursão histórica à crise terminal do regime,* Master's Thesis in Contemporary History (Lisbon: Faculdade de Ciências Sociais e Humanas, Universidade Nova de Lisboa, 2012)

Osório, Sanches, *O Equívoco do 25 de Abril* (Lisbon: Editorial Intervenção, 1975)

Pereira, António Maria, *A Burla do 28 de Setembro* (Lisbon: Livraria Bertrand, 1976)

Pinto, Pedro Feytor, *Na Sombra do Poder* (Lisbon: Publicações D. Quixote, 2011)

Pontes, Joana, Castro, Rodrigo de Sousa e, Afonso, Aniceto, *A Hora da Liberdade. O 25 de Abril, pelos protagonistas* (Lisbon: Editorial Bizâncio, 2012)

Ramos, Armando, "Todos os anos celebro com a mesma alegria o 16 de Março e o 25 de Abril", *Gazeta das Caldas*, April 22, 2011

Rebello, Augusto de Sá Viana, *Salazar e Caetano Falar Claro* (Lisbon: Nova Arrancada, 2003)

Rocha, João Manuel, "Guiné-Bissau – Os camaradas estão a perguntar se é assim que se toma a independência", *Público* newspaper, September 24, 2013

Rodrigues, Paulo Madeira, *De Súbito em Abril, 24, 25, 26* (Lisbon: Arcádia, 1974)

Rodrigues, Avelino et al. *O Movimento dos Capitães e o 25 de Abril*, 5ª edition (Lisbon: Planeta, 2014)

Santos, Bruno Oliveira, *Histórias Secretas da PIDE/DGS* (Lisbon: Nova Arrancada, 2000)

Santos, Garcia dos Santos [et al.], *As transmissões militares: Da Guerra Peninsular ao 25 de Abril* (Lisbon: Commission for the History of Transmissions, 2008)

Serrão, Hélder da Silva, *CIOE/CTOE – Operações Especiais – 50 anos* (Lamego: Edições Esgotadas, 2011)

Serrão, Joaquim Veríssimo, *Marcello Caetano – Confidências no Exílio* (Lisbon: Editorial Verbo, 1985)

Serrão, Joaquim Veríssimo, *Correspondência com Marcello Caetano – 1974-1980* (Venda Nova: Bertrand Editora, 1994)

Sieve, Harold, "Portuguese 'coup' ends in fiasco. "*The Sunday Telegraph*, March 17, 1974

Sieve, Harold, "Portuguese purge of armed forces continues." *The Daily Telegraph*, March 19, 1974

Sieve, Harold, "Purge of Portuguese Army extended." *The Daily Telegraph*, March 20, 1974

Silva, Alexandre Pais Ribeiro da, *Capitães de Abril*, Vol. I (Lisbon: Amigos do Livro, Editores, 1974)

Soares, Mário, *Um político assume-se, Ensaio autobiográfico político e ideológico* (Lisbon: Temas e Debates/Círculo de Leitores, 2011)

Sousa, Pedro Marquês de, *Os Números da Guerra de África – Angola Guiné e Moçambique* (Lisbon: Guerra e Paz, 2021)

Spínola, António de, *Portugal e o Futuro*, 5th Edition (Lisbon: Arcádia, 1974)

Spínola, António de, *País sem rumo – Contributo para a História de uma Revolução* (Lisbon: SCIRE, 1978)

Tal, David, *Symbol Not Substance? Israel's Campaign to Acquire Hawk Missiles, 1960-1962*, The International History Review Vol. 22, No. 2 (Jun. 2000)

Tavares-Teles, António, *Otelo – 18 de Janeiro* (Lisbon: Author's Edition, 1976)

Thomaz, Américo, *Últimas décadas de Portugal*, Vol. IV (Lisbon: Fernando Pereira Editor, 1983)

Tíscar, Maria José, *A Pide no Xadrez Africano – Conversas com o inspector Fragoso Allas*, 2nd edition (Lisbon: Edições Colibri, 2018)

Tornada, Joana de Matos, *Nas vésperas da democracia em Portugal, o golpe das Caldas de 16 de Março* (Coimbra: Almedina, 2009)

Ulanoff, Stanley M. and Eshel, David, *The Fighting Israeli Air Force – The Amazing Combat History of the World's Finest Air Force 1948-1984* (New York: Arco Publishing, INC, 1985)

Vasco, Nuno, *Vigiados e perseguidos. Documentos Secretos da PIDE/DGS* (Amadora: Livraria Bertrand, 1977)

Vieira, Joaquim, *Mário Soares, uma vida* (biografia revista e ampliada), volume 2 (edited for Sábado magazine) (Lisboa: Reverso, 2022)

Villas-Boas, José Manuel, *Caderno de Memórias* (Lisbon: Temas e Debates, 2003)

NOTES

Chapter 1

1. Caetano, *Depoimento*, p. 200. As shown in Volume 1, the book had been published in February 1974 and caused a political earthquake by questioning the regime's policy in Africa.
2. Thomaz, *Últimas Décadas de Portugal*, p. 351.
3. Thomaz, p. 352.
4. Caetano, *Depoimento*, p. 200.
5. Thomaz, pp. 352–353.
6. Mello, Manuel José Homem de, *Meio Século de Observação*, p. 212.
7. AMC/12-809: Summary records of the meeting held at the Department of National Defence on 11 March 1974. Office of the Secretary of State for the Army, Box. 33, no. 3.
8. ADN/GABMIN/007/0029/006: Letter from the Commander-in-Chief of the Armed Forces in Guinea to the Minister of National Defence, Bissau, March 12, 1974.
9. As shown in Volume 1, Portugal had received a loan of 150 million rands from South Africa to spend on arms.
10. AHD – PAA 960, 18 Pack 1140: Letter from the Portuguese Minister of Defence to the South African Minister of Defence, Lisbon, March 4, 1974.
11. Loudon, Bruce, "Portuguese forces put on alert", *The Sunday Telegraph*, March 10, 1974, p. 36.
12. Loudon, Bruce, "Africa War Crisis Grips Portugal", *The Daily Telegraph*, March 11, 1974, p. 32.
13. AMC/PC-UTL/01: Letter from Luís C. Lupi to Prof. Marcello Caetano, on the role played by the English journalist Bruce Loudon, Lisbon, March 12, 1974, President of the Council, Ultramar/Reports notes and correspondence, 1968-1974, Box. 12, no. 12.
14. Caetano, *Depoimento*, p. 200.
15. The National Assembly was controlled by a single party, which always supported the government, and Américo Thomaz had little choice in 1974 to replace Caetano.
16. Caetano, *Depoimento*, p. 201.
17. Cruzeiro, *Costa Gomes, o último Marechal*, p. 206.
18. Lemos, *Duas crises*, p. 80.
19. Cruzeiro, *Costa Gomes, o último Marechal*, p. 206.
20. Spínola, *País sem rumo*, pp. 79–80.
21. Lemos, *Duas crises*, pp. 83–85. In this conversation, Costa Gomes seems to show that the only problem he had with the ceremony was to appear in public with other generals to confirm government policy. But as we saw earlier, Costa Gomes had told Silva Cunha that he did not agree with the continuation of the war and that the problem of Overseas Territories had to have a political solution.
22. Caetano, *Depoimento*, p. 201.
23. Spínola, *País sem rumo*, p. 79. In an interview with José Manuel Barroso in *Segredos de Abril* (Lisbon: Editorial Notícias, 1995) p. 72, Costa Gomes stated that 'in the conversation he had with us, before dismissing us, he said that one of us should claim the position of head of government,' seemingly referring to the conversation of 13 March. But as the two were received separately on that day it is likely that Costa Gomes was referring to the conversation in late February in which Caetano made that statement. On the other hand, since Marcello had already twice asked Thomaz to resign, and he did not accept the request, it did not make much sense to offer power to the two generals on the eve of exonerating them.
24. Besides the absence of Costa Gomes, Spínola and Bagulho, General Silvino Silvério Marques, who was in the Direction of Instruction in the Army General Staff, was also absent, justifying his absence by having at that time an audience with Américo Thomaz in Belém Palace, Cf. Caetano, *Depoimento*, p. 202, although this was not true. In his book, *Marcello Caetano, Angola e o 25 de Abril – Uma Polémica com Veríssimo Serrão* (Mem Martins: Editorial Inquérito, 1995), p. 20, Silvério Marques confesses that he was absent because he strongly disagreed with Caetano's overseas policy and that he told this to the Army Minister, General Andrade e Silva, adding that he had an audience with Thomaz that day. Later when he got home, he realised he had made a mistake, but no longer corrected the error. Another who was absent was Brigadier Jaime Silvério Marques (brother of General Silvino), who was Director of the Military Transport Services and who would also have been present at the audience with Américo Thomaz, although no such audience took place that day. Also conspicuous by his absence was General Kaúlza de Arriaga, who was also plotting against Marcello Caetano, but for reasons opposite to the movement of the captains.
25. https://www.youtube.com/watch?v=DML8XXPsCC0
26. Rodrigues, Paulo Madeira, *De Súbito em Abril, 24, 25, 26*, pp. 17–20.
27. *Diário Popular* newspaper, March 15, 1974, pp. 1–9.
28. Caetano, *Depoimento*, pp. 202–203.
29. Lemos, *Duas crises*, p. 86
30. Elmano Alves in Cruz, Manuel Braga da, Ramos, Rui (org.), *Marcello Caetano – Tempos de Transição*, pp. 145–146.

31 In a letter to Joaquim Veríssimo Serrão in 1979, Caetano mentions that the resignation of Costa Gomes and Spínola was inevitable, but that he tried to avoid the crisis he knew would arise because of this, implying that he did everything to avoid the resignation of the two military chiefs, which seems to confirm Thomaz's perception on the matter. Cf. Serrão, *Correspondence with Marcello Caetano – 1974-1980*, p. 237.
32 The Silvério Marque's brothers, who had a meeting with Thomaz that day.
33 Thomaz, p. 354.
34 Archives du MAE, FR MAE 200QO, Direction Europe, Portugal 1971-1976, Politique intérieure 130, série 28, sous série 3, dossier 1, 1974, Ambassade de France au Portugal, Télégramme n° 72-75, Lisbonne, le 15 mars 1974. Bernard Durand, Ambassador of France in Portugal, to his Excellency, the Minister for Foreign Affairs.
35 Caetano, *Depoimento*, p. 200.
36 AMC/PC/05: Speeches and interviews 1972-1974, Inauguration speech, after Government reshuffle, Cx 13, no. 14.
37 Archives du MAE, FR MAE 200QO, Direction Europe, Portugal 1971-1976, Politique intérieure 130, série 28, sous série 3, dossier 1, 1974, Ambassade de France au Portugal, Lettre nº 274, Lisbonne, le 13 mars 1974. Bernard Durand, Ambassadeur de France au Portugal, à son Excellence Monsieur le ministre des Affaires étrangères.
38 Archives du MAE, FR MAE 200QO, Direction Europe, Portugal 1971-1976, Politique intérieure 130, série 28, sous série 3, dossier 1, 1974, Ambassade de France au Portugal, Télégramme n° 66-69, Lisbonne, le 13 mars 1974. Bernard Durand, Ambassador of France in Portugal, to his Excellency, the Minister for Foreign Affairs.
39 *Central Intelligence Bulletin,* March 15, 1974, CIA-RDP-79T00975A026200001-8, CIA Records Search Tool (CREST), National Archives and Records Administration. https://www.cia.gov/readingroom/docs/CIA-RDP79T00975A026200200001-8.pdf
40 Amaral, Diogo Freitas do, *O Antigo Regime e a Revolução Memórias Políticas*, p. 134.

Chapter 2

1 Almeida, Dinis, *Origens e evolução do Movimento de Capitães: subsídios para uma melhor compreensão*, p. 278.
2 Kaúlza da Arriaga refers in his book *Guerra e Política. Em Nome da Verdacde. Os Anos Decisivos,* p. 64, that in the conversation he had with Marcello Caetano, he did not hide anything from him and that he said he belonged to a group of generals that aimed at replacing the government. In a letter to Joaquim Veríssimo Serrão in 1979, Marcello Caetano speaks of a meeting with Kaúlza on 14 February 1974 (the date may be in error), in which he confronted him with news that he was conspiring against the government. Kaúlza was embarrassed and denied that he was conspiring, admitting only that he had spoken with two or three generals to see what could be done about the discontent of the captains. Serrão, *Correspondência com Marcello Caetano 1974-1980*, p. 239. Cunha, *Ainda o 25 de Abril*, pp. 86–91.
3 Carvalho, Otelo Saraiva de, *O dia inicial. 25 de Abril. Hora a Hor* (Lisbon: Editora Objectiva, 2011), p. 261
4 Carvalho, *O dia inicial. 25 de Abril*, p. 262.
5 Serrão, Hélder da Silva, *CIOE/CTOE – Operações Especiais – 50 anos*, pp. 106–109.
6 Costeira, Arnaldo, *Eu Capitão de Abril me confesso*, pp. 43–44.
7 Colonel Sanches da Gama, who was commander of the Espinho Infantry Regiment, was relieved of his duties for showing solidarity with his officers. The same happened to Colonel Lauchener Fernandes, who commanded Cavalry Regiment 6, in Oporto. Azeredo, Carlos de Azeredo, *Trabalhos e Dias de Um Soldado do Império,* pp. 153–155.
8 Tornada, Joana de Matos, *Nas vésperas da democracia em Portugal, o golpe das Caldas de 16 de Março* (Coimbra: Almedina, 2009), pp. 65–66.
9 Bernardo, Joaquim Manuel Correia, *Santarém. Uma cidade que faz História. 25 de Abril de 1974* (Santarém: Centro de Investigação Professor Doutor Joaquim Veríssimo Serrão, 2015), pp. 119–123.
10 Carvalho, *O dia inicial. 25 de Abril*, pp. 244–250.
11 Tornada, p. 68.
12 Bernardo, *Santarém*, p. 398.
13 Spínola, *País Sem Rumo*, pp. 97–98.
14 Carvalho, *O dia inicial. 25 de Abril*, pp. 261–262.
15 The expression he used in the phone call 'we are on wheels' meant that they were ready to receive orders from the movement and get ready to leave, but not that they were about to leave. It seems that Monge understood that Lamego was about to leave when this was not true. Cf. Serrão, *Operações Especiais*, p. 258.
16 Arnaldo Costeira, who was in the RI 14 in Viseu, tells in his memoirs, *Eu Capitão de Abril me confesso* (Porto: Lello Editores, 1999), p. 43, that on the 15th, just after midday, he received a phone call from Lamego from Captain Monteiro Valente saying that they were going to leave with a force towards Lisbon and that they wanted the RI 14 not to interfere with such a movement. This contact indicates that there was indeed a willingness in Lamego to leave with forces that later did not materialise. But it was this phone call that later motivated the captains of Viseu to take a similar position. In an interview with Hélder da Silva Serrão, Monteiro Valente confirms this phone call and assumes he also called Lisbon and Porto but denies any readiness of CIOE forces to leave Lamego. He also mentions that on the night of 15 March news reached the barracks of Santa Cruz in Lamego that someone in Lisbon asked the CIOE for forces to advance on the capital, a request that was received with great perplexity, since it made no sense for Lamego to send forces so far away. Cf. Serrão, *Operações Especiais*, pp. 253–254.
17 Bernardo, *Santarém*, p. 236.
18 Bernardo, *Santarém*, pp. 240–243.
19 Serrão, *Operações Especiais*, p. 262.
20 Vasco Lourenço, in an interview with Maria Manuela Cruzeiro, mentions that Otelo was unable to resist the pressure from Spínola's men in the face of the resignation of the two generals and agreed to participate in the coup with the support of other elements of the MFA. Otelo's involvement then facilitated contacts within the units, namely in Caldas, where there was a strong core of MFA officers, who when they realised that Otelo was involved decided to join so as not to be accused of boycotting the action. Cf. Cruzeiro, *Vasco Lourenço, do Interior da Revolução*, pp. 193–194.
21 Carvalho, *O dia inicial. 25 de Abril*, pp. 262–264.
22 Manuel Monge in *Pronunciamento Militar do 25 de Abril de 1974*, V Conference of the Núcleo Impulsionador das Conferências da Cooperativa Militar (NICCM), NICCM Edition, 2014, p. 101. The alert was given by the commander of the Student Body of the Military Academy, Colonel Leopoldo Severo, who, after the cadets' party, saw officers at the Academy who were strangers to the institution and reported the situation to Viana de Lemos. Lemos, *Duas crises*, p. 89; Carvalho, *O dia inicial. 25 de Abril*, p. 269.
23 Spínola, *País sem rumo*, pp. 98–99.
24 This statement by Spínola results from a conversation he had with Costa Gomes and actually corresponds to a support expressed by Romeiras to Costa Gomes when the general was removed from the post of CEMGFA. On that day, Romeiras phoned him to say that he agreed 'two hundred per cent' with the attitude that Costa Gomes had taken by not attending the ceremony supporting the Government's policy. However, the fact that he agreed with the attitude towards the act, did not mean that Romeiras was available to participate in a military revolt. Cf. Letter from António Varela Romeiras Júnior published in the newspaper *O Dia* on 9 February 1979, p. 13.
25 Manuel Monge in *Pronunciamento Militar do 25 de Abril de 1974*, V Conference of the Núcleo Impulsionador das Conferências da Cooperativa Militar (NICCM), NICCM Edition, 2014, p. 102.
26 Otelo says that it was Monge and Casanova who went to RC 7 to ask for protection for Costa Gomes and Spínola. See Carvalho, *O dia inicial. 25 de Abril*, p. 270. Spínola states that he was visited that night by Monge and Jaime Neves and, a little later, by Almeida Bruno, and that the latter informed him that Costa Gomes was staying overnight in RC 7. Spínola, *País sem rumo*, p. 99. Thus, after having been at Spínola's house, Monge and Jaime Neves went to RC 7 to ask for Costa Gomes' protection so that he could be taken to the barracks. Cf. Manuel Monge in *Pronunciamento Militar do 25 de Abril de 1974*, V Conferência do Núcleo Impulsionador das Conferências da Cooperativa Militar (NICCM), NICCM Edition, 2014, p. 102.
27 Lemos, *Duas crises*, pp. 89–90. Romeiras found the request very strange, due to the fact that he was a friend of Costa Gomes and Costa Gomes had not contacted him personally to ask for any kind of protection.
28 Otelo and Miquelina Simões narrowly escaped this raid, because when they were passing by the building where Monge lived they saw the PIDE/DGS agents arriving. Cf. Carvalho, *O dia inicial. 25 de Abril*, p. 271.
29 Lemos, *Duas crises*, p. 91.
30 In an interview with Bruno Oliveira Santos in *Histórias Secretas da PIDE/DGS* (Lisbon: Nova Arrancada, 2000), p. 150, Óscar Cardoso clearly states that the order to arrest Monge and also Almeida Bruno came from the military, although he does not identify which military entity that order came from.
31 Carvalho, *O dia inicial. 25 de Abril*, pp. 268–274.
32 Ramos, Armando, "Todos os anos celebro com a mesma alegria o 16 de Março e o 25 de Abril", *Gazeta das Caldas*, April 22, 2011.
33 Rodrigues, Avelino et al. *O Movimento dos Capitães e o 25 de Abril*, p. 119.
34 Coelho, Adelino de Matos, "Sobre o 16 de Março de 1974", *Gazeta das Caldas*, April 28, 2022.
35 *Diário de Notícias* newspaper, March 17, 1974.
36 Carvalho, *O dia inicial. 25 de Abril*, pp. 274–275.
37 Manuel Monge in *Pronunciamento Militar do 25 de Abril de 1974*, V Conference of the Núcleo Impulsionador das Conferências da Cooperativa Militar (NICCM), NICCM Edition, 2014, p. 104.
38 Since 1956, the Central Airborne Warning Command was installed at the top of Monsanto Forest Park, in Lisbon. The 1st Air Region Command had its headquarters here along with the Air Defence Command. In the late 1960s a new building was built for the 1st Airborne Region Command,

39. Caetano, *Depoimento,* p. 203. The defence of Monsanto should be ensured by paratroopers coming from Tancos, but according to Marcello these forces would never arrive, claiming that a dense fog prevented their departure from Tancos by helicopter. Cf. *Marcello Caetano. O 25 de Abril e o Ultramar. Três entrevistas e alguns documentos,* Lisbon: Verbo, s.d. p. 77. Silva Cunha says that the security of this unit was later ensured by GNR forces. Cunha, *Ainda o 25 de Abril,* p. 115.
40. Thomaz, pp. 356–357.
41. ADN/GABMIN/007/0029/007: Letter from the Minister of National Defence to the Commander-in-Chief of the Guinean Armed Forces, March 21, 1974.
42. Marques, *Portugal, e Agora?,* p. 203.
43. There is no reliable information that the Air Force was mobilised that day. The only information we have on the possible use of helicopters comes from Otelo Saraiva de Carvalho, who states that the Army Minister, Andrade e Silva, asked the Secretary of State for Aeronautics, Tello Polleri, to order an Alouette III from Tancos Air Base 3, armed with cannon, to sweep the column from Caldas, a request that Polleri refused. Cf. Carvalho, *Alvorada em Abril,* p. 284.
44. Caetano, *Depoimento* , p. 204.
45. Caetano, *Depoimento* , p. 204.
46. Carvalho, *Alvorada em Abril,* pp. 282–283.
47. Manuel Monge in *Pronunciamento Militar do 25 de Abril de 1974,* V Conferência do Núcleo Impulsionador das Conferências da Cooperativa Militar (NICCM) (Lisbon: NICCM Edition, 2014), pp. 104–105
48. Interview given by Luís Piedade Faria to Fernanda Mestrinho and Diana Andringa, in the RTP programme held to commemorate the 25th anniversary of the 25th of April. Part 1, April 25, 1999. https://arquivos.rtp.pt/conteudos/25-de-abril-parte-i/
49. Serrão, *Operações Especiais,* p. 263.
50. Serrão, *Operações Especiais,* p. 255.
51. Carvalho, *Alvorada em Abril,* p. 277.
52. Costa, *Eu Capitão de Abril, me confesso,* p. 47.
53. Santos, *Histórias Secretas da PIDE/DGS,* p. 145.
54. ADN/GABMIN/055/0307/032: Messages sent. There is no record of any measures taken on national territory in the files of the minister's office when the authors of this book consulted them.
55. ADN/GABMIN/055/0307/033: Messages received
56. Brito, Carlos, *Álvaro Cunhal Sete fôlegos de um combatente* (Lisbon: Edições Nelson de Matos, 2010), pp. 72–75.
57. Brito, pp. 79–80.
58. This statement is reproduced by José Freire Antunes in *Os Americanos e Portugal* Vol. I *Os anos de Richard Nixon 1969-1974* (Lisbon: Publicações Dom Quixote, 1986), p.296, however, it was not possible to find Rabenold's statement in the original document. Cf. The Complex of United States – Portugal Relations Before and After the Coup, Hearings Before the Subcommittee on Africa of the Committee on Foreign Affairs, House of Representatives, Ninety-Third Congress. Second Sessions. Mar. 14; Oct. 8, 9, and 22, 1974 by United States. Congress. House. Foreign Affairs. 1974.
59. Soares, Mário, *Um político assume-se, Ensaio autobiográfico político e ideológico* (Lisbon: Temas e Debates/Círculo de Leitores, 2011), pp. 168–169.
60. Vieira, Joaquim, *Mário Soares, uma vida* (biografia revista e ampliada), volume 2 (edited for Sábado magazine) (Lisboa: Reverso, 2022), pp.104–105.
61. Gomes, Bernardino and Sá, Tiago Moreira de, *Carlucci vs Kissinger – Os EUA e a Revolução Portuguesa* (Lisbon: Dom Quixote, 2008), pp. 15–16.
62. AMC/12-859: Letter from Marcello Caetano to Laureano López Rodó, 20-03-1974, Box. 34, Correspondence/López Rodó, Laureano, no. 128.
63. ADN/GABMIN/007/0037/060.
64. Villas-Boas, José Manuel, *Caderno de Memórias* (Lisbon: Temas e Debates, 2003), p.106.
65. Loudon, Bruce, "How the mighty pen split Portugal" *The Sunday Telegraph,* March 17, 1974, p. 21.
66. AMC/12-1254: Letter from Bruce S. Loudon to Pedro Feytor Pinto, concerning the unpleasant reaction of the Secretary of State for Information and Tourism to an article of his authorship published in *The Sunday Telegraph,* Estoril, March 27, 1974, Box.45, Correspondence/Pinto, no. 11, Annex 1.
67. AMC/12-1254: Letter concerning the article by Bruce S. Loudon, published in *The Sunday Telegraph* newspaper on 17 March 1974, Lisbon, March 27, 1974, Box.45, Correspondence/Pinto, no. 11.
68. Sieve, Harold, "Portuguese 'coup' ends in fiasco." *The Sunday Telegraph,* March 17, 1974, pp. [1]+
69. Sieve, Harold, "Portuguese purge of armed forces continues." *The Daily Telegraph,* March 19, 1974, p. 4.
70. Sieve, Harold, "Purge of Portuguese Army extended." *The Daily Telegraph,* March 20, 1974, p. 4. This situation had happened with a company led by Lieutenant Colonel Luís Ataíde Banazol, who had refused to go to Guinea, and the company was then divided to avoid further problems.
71. Archives du MAE, FR MAE 200QO, Direction Europe, Portugal 1971-1976, Politique intérieure 130, série 28, sous série 3, dossier 1, 1974, Ambassade de France au Portugal, Télégramme n° 89-92, Lisbonne, le 21 mars 1974. Bernard Durand, Ambassador of France in Portugal, to his Excellency, Minister for Foreign Affairs.
72. Archives du MAE, FR MAE 200QO, Direction Europe, Portugal 1971-1976, Politique intérieure 130, série 28, sous série 3, dossier 1, 1974, Ambassade de France au Portugal, Lettre n° 278, Lisbonne, le 29 mars 1974. Bernard Durand, Ambassadeur de France au Portugal, à son Excellence Monsieur le ministre des Affaires étrangères.
73. ANTT: Definitive Archives Division/Fund: Ministry of the Interior/Subfund: Office of the Minister (1948-1977); Book 66 record of correspondence received (no. 1232-2298) 1974, Jan.-Mar. – NT 53.
74. ANTT: Definitive Archives Division/Fund: Ministry of the Interior/Subfund: Office of the Minister (1948-1977); Copy of Outgoing Correspondence no. (601-1200) 1974 ref MAI pt 199.
75. Villas-Boas, p. 101. See also Castanheira, José Pedro, "The meeting that came too late", Expresso Magazine No. 1117 of 26 March 1994, pp. 30–42.
76. ADN/SGDN/2REP/078/0329/007: Report on the visit to Guinea of the Military Attaché, Colonel Huggan, and 1st Secretary Gerald Clark, from the British Embassy, Lisbon, Bissau, 9 February 1974.
77. Patrício, Rui, "Política Externa Portuguesa, 1970-1974", in Cruz, Manuel Braga da and Ramos, Rui, (Org.), *Marcelo Caetano: Tempos de Transição,* 1st ed. (Porto: Porto Editora, 2012).
78. Rui Patrício's interview with Joaquim Furtado in *A Guerra,* episode 40, 2013.
79. In an interview with Joaquim Furtado, the Portuguese ambassador admitted that the offer of full independence was a lure for the ceasefire, which was what interested the Portuguese, and not exactly the independence of Guinea. On this question, Rui Patrício states that the emissary was going to London to talk and not to negotiate independence with the guerrillas. Cf. *A Guerra,* episode 40, 2013.
80. Villas-Boas, p. 104.
81. Villas-Boas, pp. 105–106.
82. Interview of Aristides Pereira to Joaquim Furtado in *A Guerra,* episode 40, 2013.
83. As we saw in the first volume, these missiles were eventually supplied covertly from Israel and were ready in Germany to be shipped when the revolution took place in Portugal.
84. Magalhães, J. Calvet de, *O 25 de Abril e as Necessidades,* Estratégia – Revista de Estudos Internacionais, IEEI, 2004, p. 5. Cf. ADN/IEEI/001/0022.
85. As seen in the first volume, in 1974 Portugal was negotiating the American stay at the Lajes base in the Azores and was seeking political and military compensations.
86. AMC/PC/02: Note 28/3/74, "Conversation with the US Embassy Counsellor", reported by Freitas Cruz, President of the Council, Negotiations with the US on the Azores, 1973-1974, Box.12, no.58.
87. Telegram 4737, American Embassy Lisbon to Department of State, December 28, 1973, "Coup Plot Foiled in Portugal", State Department, National Archives, Washington.
88. Telegram 454, American Embassy Lisbon to Department of State, February 5, 1974, "Initial Meeting with Caetano", State Department, National Archives, Washington.
89. Telegram 790, American Embassy Lisbon to Department of State, March 4, 1974, "Foreign Minister makes renewed appeal for relaxation US arms embargo", State Department, National Archives, Washington.
90. Telegram 55334, Department of State to American Embassy Lisbon, March 20, 1974, "Redeye weapons system", State Department, National Archives, Washington.
91. Telegram 1047, American Embassy Lisbon to Department of State, March 16, 1974, "Effect of Portuguese Political Crisis on Azores Negotiations", State Department, National Archives, Washington.
92. Telegram 1214, American Embassy Lisbon to Department of State, March 30, 1974, "Portugal: Political/Economic Trends, First Quarter 1974", State Department, National Archives, Washington.
93. Múrias, *De Salazar a Costa Gomes* (Lisbon: Nova Arrancada, 1998), p. 287.
94. Archives du MAE, FR MAE 200QO, Direction Europe, Portugal 1971-1976, Politique intérieure 130, série 28, sous série 3, dossier 1, 1974, Ambassade de France au Portugal, Télégramme n° 78-83, Lisbonne, le 18 mars 1974. Bernard Durand, Ambassador of France in Portugal, to his Excellency, Minister for Foreign Affairs.
95. Carvalho, *Alvorada em Abril,* pp. 289–293.
96. Carvalho, *Alvorada em Abril,* pp. 295–296.
97. Almeida, Luís Pinheiro and Cabral, Rui, *25 de Abril, memórias* (Lisbon: Agência Lusa, special edition, 1994), p. 34.
98. Almeida, *25 de Abril, memórias,* pp. 302–303.
99. Caetano, *Depoimento,* pp. 240–246. See also *Diário de Notícias* newspaper March 29, 1974

100 AMC/12-1569: Supreme Administrative Court, Letter from Judge Álvaro Rodrigues Tavares dated March 29, 1974, Correspondence/Tavares, Box. 56, no. 18.
101 AMC/12-816: Letter from Eduardo Metzner Leone dated March 29, 1974, Correspondence/Leone, Box. 33, no. 5.
102 Archives du MAE, FR MAE 200QO, Direction Europe, Portugal 1971-1976, Politique intérieure 130, série 28, sous série 3, dossier 1, 1974, Ambassade de France au Portugal, Lettre nº 405, Lisbonne, le 5 avril 1974. Bernard Durand, Ambassadeur de France au Portugal, à son Excellence Monsieur le ministre des Affaires étrangères.
103 *Diário de Notícias* newspaper, 1 April 1974.

Chapter 3

1 Carvalho, *Alvorada em Abril,* pp. 304–305. Otelo speaks of 55 vehicles of this model having been ordered, but Nuno Andrade mentions an order for 38 vehicles and the existence on 25 April of three vehicles that were operational, but which did not yet have their armaments installed. Andrade, Nuno, *Para Além do Portão. A GNR e o Carmo na Revolução de Abril* (Lisbon: Guerra e Paz, 2007), pp. 47 and 52. A later information from the General Command of the GNR dated November 26, 1975, confirms the existence of 38 vehicles, placed in a military depot in Beirolas, after the attempted military coup of 11 March 1975. Cf. ADN/CEMGFA/004/0008/039.
2 The only officer of the Regiment of Lancers 2 who sided with the MFA was Captain Campos Andrada, who acted as the regiment's security officer but was not in charge of troops and therefore had little influence over the regiment's soldiers.
3 Carvalho, *Alvorada em Abril*, p. 306.
4 ADN/CEMGFA/005/0011/019: An information from the 4th Division of the Army Staff of 7 July 1970, reported the existence of 115 M47 Pattons in the Cavalry Regiment 4 of Santa Margarida. However, of this set, only 10 M47s were operational due to the lack of funds for their maintenance. For 1974, it was not possible to find information about the number of operational M47 Pattons at Santa Margarida. Besides this unit, there were also some M47s at the Cavalry Practical School in Santarém. In 1974, this unit had five Pattons assigned, four being operational and one unable to move. Cf. Bernardo, *Santarém*, p. 195.
5 In 1965, Portugal acquired 40 Panhard AML (*Auto Mitrailleuse Légère*) HE 60-7 vehicles for cavalry units from the French. After that purchase, Portugal received on loan 32 more Panhard AML vehicles from South Africa, known in that country as Eland-60. These vehicles were the same as the French ones, with only differences in the radio equipment. Cf. Coutinho, Pereira, "Exército Português – Auto-Metralhadoras" (2nd part), *Revista da Cavalaria* no. 27, May/August 2012, p. 7.
6 ADN/SGDN/3REP/068/0173/002: PANHARD catalogues with technical drawings. The EBR was armed with the long 75mm SA 50 rifled cannon equipped with an autoloader. In addition to this version, Portugal also received 28 EBR-ETTs during 1959, which had no cannon, intended exclusively for troop transport.
7 Monteiro, Pedro, *Berliet, Chaimite e UMM – Os Grandes Veículos Militares Nacionais* (Lisbon: Contra Corrente, 2018).
8 PSP weekly PERINTREP no. 15/74 published by Editions Aphrodite in May 1974.
9 Archives du MAE, FR MAE 200QO, Direction Europe, Portugal 1971-1976, Politique intérieure 130, série 28, sous série 3, dossier 1, 1974, Ambassade de France au Portugal, Lettre no 427, Lisbonne, le 11 avril 1974. Bernard Durand, Ambassadeur de France au Portugal, à son Excellence Monsieur le ministre des Affaires étrangères.
10 Archives du MAE, FR MAE 200QO, Direction Europe, Portugal 1971-1976, Politique intérieure 130, série 28, sous série 3, dossier 1, 1974, Ambassade de France au Portugal, Lettre nº 445, Lisbonne, le 19 avril 1974. Bernard Durand, Ambassadeur de France au Portugal, à son Excellence Monsieur le ministre des Affaires étrangères.
11 Archives du MAE, FR MAE 200QO, Direction Europe, Portugal 1971-1976, Politique intérieure 130, série 28, sous série 3, dossier 1, 1974, Ambassade de France au Portugal, Lettre nº 445, Lisbonne, le 19 avril 1974. Bernard Durand, Ambassadeur de France au Portugal, à son Excellence Monsieur le ministre des Affaires étrangères. This attack on 9 April 1974 was carried out by the Revolutionary Brigades who perpetrated an attack against the ship Niassa to delay the embarkation of troops to Guinea.
12 Archives du MAE, FR MAE 200QO, Direction Europe, Portugal 1971-1976, Politique intérieure 130, série 28, sous série 3, dossier 1, 1974, Sous-Direction d`Europe Méridionale, Note, A.S/ Situation au Portugal, Paris, le 20 avril 1974.
13 Interview with Cunha Passo in *Histórias Secretas da PIDE/DGS* by Bruno Oliveira Santos (Lisbon: Nova Arrancada, 2000), p. 143.
14 Interview with Abílio Pires in *Histórias Secretas da PIDE/DGS*, pp. 145–146.
15 Interview with Óscar Cardoso in *Secret Histories of PIDE/DGS*, p. 151.
16 Ockrent, Christine, Marenches, Count Alexandre de, *No Segredo dos Deuses*, p. 160.
17 Caetano, *Depoimento*, p. 204. In the same vein is the testimony of the former Minister of the Navy, Pereira Crespo, who in his memoir's states that after the failure of Caldas on 16 March, the DGS thought that the new coup attempt would only occur a few months later. Cf. Crespo, Manuel Pereira, *Porque Perdemos a Guerra*, p. 138.
18 Carvalho, *Alvorada em Abril*, pp. 306–310.
19 Otelo Saraiva de Carvalho, Victor Crespo, Sanches Osório, Fischer Lopes Pires, Garcia dos Santos and Luís Macedo.
20 Interview of Otelo to Dominique de Roux published in the French newspaper *Le Figaro* on 30 April 1974. In this interview with the French journalist, Otelo also mentions that Spínola was not aware of the preparations for the coup and that until 25 April he was distanced from the captains' movement, which we know is not true, since Spínola was informed of the captains' movements and gave input into the preparation of the political programme.
21 The original handwritten order of operations is reproduced in several appendices of Otelo Saraiva de Carvalho's book *Alvorada em Abril*, pp. 553–589. Due to handwriting and personal notes, what Otelo wrote is not always intelligible, hence the general plan of operations has been reproduced again in a collective work coordinated by Carlos de Almada Contreiras, *Operação Viragem Histórica: 25 de Abril de 1974,* pp. 95–110.
22 Santos, Garcia dos dos [et al.], As transmissões militares: Da Guerra Peninsular ao 25 de Abril, Lisbon: Comissão da História das Transmissões, 2008, pp. 200–207; Carvalho, Alvorada em Abril, pp. 335–337. See also, A voz e os ouvidos do MFA, documentary by António-Pedro Vasconcelos and Leandro Ferreira on the operation that allowed the MFA to communicate on 25 April 1974. https://www.rtp.pt/play/p3438/e285510/a-voz-e-os-ouvidos-do-mfa
23 Almeida e Cabral, *25 de Abril, memórias*, p. 40.
24 Carvalho, *Alvorada em Abril,* pp. 315–322. Details on how the contacts and the taking over of the radios took place can be found in the book by Matos Maia, *Aqui Emissora da Liberdade: Rádio Clube Português 04.26 25 de Abril de 1974* (Lisbon: Rádio Clube Português Edition, 1975). See also Otelo Saraiva de Carvalho's testimony at the V Conference of the *Núcleo Impulsionador das Conferências da Cooperativa Militar* (NICCM) in June 2012 reproduced in *Pronunciamento Militar do 25 de Abril de 1974* (Lisbon: NICCM, 2014), pp.170–171.
25 Carvalho, Alvorada em Abril, pp. 322–323. See also the video from the RTP archives showing images of the occupation of the television studios, which took place without major incident. https://www.youtube.com/watch?v=K1B2G5BHrqs
26 Carvalho, *Alvorada em Abril*, pp. 325–326.
27 Carvalho, *Alvorada em Abril*, p. 327.
28 Carvalho, *Alvorada em Abril*, p. 327.
29 Carvalho, *Alvorada em Abril*, pp. 327–332.
30 Carvalho, *Alvorada em Abril*, p. 338.
31 In his memoirs, Spínola mentions that the first version of the document that reached his hands was of communist inspiration, but the general hoped, with Costa Gomes's support, to avoid that the movement would be dominated by the communists. Cf. Spínola, *País sem Rumo*, p. 103.
32 Carvalho, *Alvorada em Abril*, pp. 339–341.
33 Spínola, *País sem Rumo*, p. 103.
34 There is some confusion regarding the date when Costa Gomes became aware of the MFA programme. Although the general speaks of eight days before 25 April, i.e. 18 April, everything indicates that it was before the contact with Spínola on 14 April, given that Spínola later confirmed to Vasco Gonçalves that the first version of the MFA programme had been approved by Costa Gomes. Cf. Spínola, *País sem rumo*.
35 Cruzeiro, *Costa Gomes: O último marechal,* pp. 201, 211–212.
36 Nuno Vasco refers in his book *Vigiados e perseguidos. Documentos Secretos da PIDE/DGS* (Amadora: Livraria Bertrand, 1977), p. 17, that Costa Gomes and António de Spínola were indeed bugged on 24 April, but he does not provide any proof in this respect.
37 Carvalho, *Alvorada em Abril*, pp.351–352. See also Golias, Jorge Sales, *A Descolonização da Guiné-Bissau e o Movimento dos Capitães,* 2nd edition (Lisbon: Edições Colibri, 2017), pp. 110–111.
38 Bernardo, *Santarém*, pp. 162–163.
39 Jardim, *Moçambique – Terra Queimada*, pp. 93–98.
40 Jardim, annexed documents, p. 417 ff. See also AMC/12-752: Contacts with Zambia, with two documents attached, Correspondence with Jorge Pereira Jardim, Box. 32, No. 177, Annexes 1 and 2.
41 In an interview with the Brazilian newspaper *O Mundo Português* in 1976, Marcello Caetano clearly stated that he never authorised any initiative to allow negotiations with FRELIMO and that Jardim had abused his contacts with Kaunda. Cf. Caetano, *O 25 de Abril e o Ultramar…*, p. 71. However, the possibility of white independence in Mozambique would not be completely ruled out in the plans of the government in Lisbon. There is a report that the Minister of Overseas Territories, Baltazar Rebelo de Sousa, had discreetly gone to Mozambique a few weeks before the military coup to assess the chances of success of a white independence in the

	colony, but concluded that such an initiative would have no future. Cf. Lã, *Do Outro Lado das Coisas – (In)Confidências Diplomáticas,* p. 122.
42	See in this regard the article by João Fernandes in the *Jornal de Macau* of April 20, 1995, reproduced in the book by Silvino Silvério Marques, *Marcello Caetano, Angola, e o 25 de Abril – Uma Polémica com Veríssimo Serrão,* pp. 83–86 and also the letter by Joaquim Mendes in the same book, pp. 78–79.
43	AMC/12-1550: Copy of a letter from the Governor-General of Angola to Baltazar Rebelo de Sousa, on the forthcoming visit of Professor Marcello Caetano to Angola, Luanda, April 10, 1974. Correspondence with Baltazar Rebelo de Sousa, Box. 55, no. 46. In an interview with the newspaper *Diário de Notícias on* May 27, 2005, Walter Marques, who was responsible for Angola's finances at the time, said that the only thing Santos e Castro told him and his colleagues in the colonial government was that the 'visit was related to the political evolution of Angola, and that this would translate into something very close to greater autonomy vis-à-vis the metropolis, as was said at the time.' However, ambassador João Rosa Lã, who lived with Santos e Castro in Caracas, Venezuela, after 25 April, says that the latter confided in him that 'in the early days of 1974,' he had been 'called to Lisbon, secretly, by the then President of the Council.' He spent an afternoon with Marcello Caetano, in a 'private car, without any escort or security,' driving around the capital and its surroundings and that, in view of the 'very dark scenario of the country's situation and of the overseas policy,' Caetano asked him to 'take all measures to prepare a unilateral declaration of independence of the territory.' Once independence was declared, Santos e Castro would be 'temporarily in charge of the new country, with a government presided over by a black personality, most probably Jonas Savimbi.' Obviously, Portugal would not accept independence, but neither would it act militarily against the rebellious colony. Cf. Lã, *Do Outro Lado das Coisas – (In)Confidências Diplomáticas,* pp. 119–120.
44	In an interview to the Brazilian newspaper *O Mundo Português* on June 25, 1976, Marcello Caetano stated that, keeping the pace of development that it had, Angola could become independent around 1976/77. Caetano, *O 25 de Abril e o Ultramar...,* p. 19.
45	Testimony of Soares Carneiro in the panel dedicated to Angola in the General Studies of Arrábida on August 31, 1995.
46	Caetano, *O 25 de Abril e o Ultramar...,* p. 119.
47	Archives du MAE, FR MAE 200QO, Direction Europe, Portugal, Relations politiques franco-portugaises, 186-191, Visite à Paris de Rui Patrício, ministre portugais des Affaires étrangères, les 7 et 8 janvier 1974, 187, série 28, sous série 24, dossier 1, Direction des Affaires Africaines et Malgaches, Note, Question des territoires portugais d`outre-mer, 20 décembre 1973.
48	Archives du MAE, FR MAE 200QO, Direction Europe, Portugal, Relations politiques franco-portugaises, 186-191, Visite à Paris de Rui Patrício, ministre portugais des Affaires étrangères, les 7 et 8 janvier 1974, 187, série 28, sous série 24, dossier 1, Direction des Affaires Politiques Europe, Compte-Rendu des entretiens sur l`Afrique et les organisations internationales.
49	Archives du MAE, FR MAE 200QO, Direction Europe, Portugal, Relations politiques franco-portugaises, 186-191, Visite à Paris de Rui Patrício, ministre portugais des Affaires étrangères, les 7 et 8 janvier 1974, 187, série 28, sous série 24, dossier 1, Directeur des Affaires Politiques, note pour le ministre, 8 janvier 1974.
50	Pinto, *Na Sombra do Poder,* pp. 259–260.
51	Castanheira, José Pedro, "Conversations in Rome", Expresso Magazine no. 1226, April 27, 1996.
52	Carvalho, *Alvorada em Abril,* p. 359.
53	Statement by Miguel Caetano to Zélia Oliveira, 2012.
54	*República* newspaper of 24 April 1974.
55	Crespo, *Porque Perdemos a Guerra,* p. 139.
56	Mello, *Meio Século de Observação,* p. 193.
57	Archives du MAE, FR MAE 200QO, Direction Europe, Portugal, Politique intérieure, carton nº 3493. Ambassade de France au Portugal, Télégramme No 122-126, Lisbonne, 24 April 1974. Bernard Durand, Ambassadeur de France au Portugal, à son Excellence Monsieur le ministre des Affaires étrangères. For more details on the negotiation of the Mirage see the articles by José Matos in *Mais Alto* magazine No. 400 (Nov/Dec 2012), pp. 37–41 and *Mais Alto* No. 401(Jan/Feb 2013), pp. 25–29 and also the article by Helena Pereira in the *Público* newspaper of 17 May 2021, pp. 12–13, on the purchase of 32 Mirage for use in Guinea.
58	Testimony by Pedro Feytor Pinto at the V Conference of the Núcleo Impulsionador das Conferências da Cooperativa Militar (NICCM) in June 2012 reproduced in *Pronunciamento Militar do 25 de Abril de 1974,* Lisbon: NICCM, 2014, pp. 50–51. See also *Na Sombra do Poder,* p. 261.
59	Thomaz, pp. 372–373.
60	Jardim, *Moçambique – Terra Queimada,* pp. 213–214.
61	Carvalho, *Alvorada em Abril,* p. 360. In his memoirs, Spínola mentions that he had already received the information of the coup that night from Major Carlos Alexandre de Morais before Ramos arrived home with more information. Cf. Spínola, *País sem Rumo,* p. 113. In fact, Carlos Morais confirms that on the night of 24 April he was warned personally by Otelo that the coup would take place that night and that he should inform General Spínola. Cf. Morais, *António de Spínola – O Homem,* p. 75.
62	Carvalho, *Alvorada em Abril,* pp. 360–364.
63	https://www.youtube.com/watch?v=-BcYhcFseWo
64	Almeida, *Origens e Evolução do Movimento dos Capitães,* pp. 351–354.
65	The chronology of these first movements is well explained in Otelo Saraiva de Carvalho's book, *O dia inicial. 25 de Abril. Hora a Hora* (Lisbon: Editora Objectiva, 2011), pp. 51–70. See also the documentary by Ginette Lavigne, *A noite do golpe de Estado,* 2001. https://www.youtube.com/watch?v=gNJEmXS58Ng
66	Bernardo, *Santarém,* p. 158.
67	Bernardo, *Santarém,* p. 182.
68	Bernardo, *Santarém,* pp. 186–189. In addition to the 232 elements from the two main groups, we must also consider the men from the health support, the civilian vehicle, and the command vehicle. This brings the total number of participants to 244. Bernardo, *Santarém,* pp. 297–302.
69	In 1954–1955 a number of Panhard EBR armoured vehicles were fitted with a 75mm cannon to improve their firepower. The modernised armoured vehicles were supplied to the French Army and also to the Portuguese Army.
70	Inside the Ford Escort were three aspirants: João Mota de Oliveira, Augusto Calado and António Laranjeira. In the car they carried a radio to communicate any hostile movement. https://www.cmjornal.pt/domingo/detalhe/uma-revolucao-a-civil
71	Maia, Salgueiro, *Capitão de Abril. Histórias da Guerra do Ultramar e do 25 de Abril* (Lisbon: Editorial News, 1997), p. 88. As regards the number of soldiers, there are publications that point to 240 men in the group that left Santarém, counting the drivers and nurses. But this number also seems to be wrong, given the number of vehicles in question (26). Cf. AAVV, *25 de Abril, Os 240 que prenderam Caetano, A coluna militar da EPC* (Lisbon: Special Edition of the Público newspaper on the 25th anniversary of the 25th of April 1999), p. 29. The journey to Lisbon was made at an average speed of 60km/h, which represented a great effort for the vehicles. Only one had problems, an old Fox armoured car commanded by furriel (junior non-commissioned officer, OR-5) Júlio de Matos, which had a flat tyre on its way to the capital and was left behind. Cf. Júnior, J. Plácido, "25 de Abril: A história nunca contada dos três azarados da coluna de Salgueiro Maia", *Visão* magazine, May 1, 2021 https://visao.sapo.pt/atualidade/sociedade/2021-05-01-25-de-abril-a-historia-nunca-contada-dos-tres-azarados-da-coluna-de-salgueiro-maia/
72	See Ponces de Carvalho's account in *Operation Historical Turn: 25 April 1974,* 2nd edition, Lisbon: Edições Colibri, 2018, pp. 431–432.
73	Almeida, *Origens e Evolução do Movimento dos Capitães,* pp. 381–386.
74	Almeida, *Origens e Evolução do Movimento dos Capitães,* pp. 394–400.
75	Costeira, *Eu Capitão de Abril me confesso,* pp. 52–53.
76	Almeida, *Origens e Evolução do Movimento dos Capitães,* pp. 344–350.
77	Almeida e Cabral, *25 de Abril, memórias,* pp. 60–61.
78	Almeida e Cabral, *25 de Abril, memórias,* pp. 52–53.
79	Serrão, *Operações Especiais,* pp. 111–117.
80	The time sequence of events in Porto is described in Carlos Azeredo's book, *Trabalhos e Dias de um Soldado do Império,* pp. 155–160. See also Almeida, *Origens e Evolução do Movimento dos Capitães,* pp. 390–394.
81	Maia, Matos, *Aqui Emissora da Liberdade: Rádio Clube Português 04.26 25 de Abril de 1974,* pp. 37–45.
82	Almeida, *Origens e Evolução do Movimento dos Capitães,* pp. 343–344.
83	Almeida e Cabral, *25 de Abril, memórias,* pp. 58–59.
84	Carvalho, *O dia inicial. 25 de Abril.,* pp. 384–385.
85	In an interview for the newspaper *Tal & Qual* on 25 April 1985, the former PIDE/DGS inspector, Pereira de Carvalho, says that the political police were not taken by surprise and that they only did not know the day, the time, and the plot of the rebellion. According to Pereira de Carvalho those who were distracted were the rulers, because in the afternoon of 24 April, Viana de Lemos, was alerted that important means of radio communication were being diverted from the Cascais barracks and that something strange was happening in the Santarém barracks. Pereira de Carvalho also mentions that after the Caldas revolt, the DGS's attention (by order of the Minister of Defence) was drawn to the possibility of a coup coming from the more conservative military sectors linked to the right-wing of the regime. Silva Pais in a written interview to *Sempre Fixe* on 19 October 1974, stated that the DGS could not act against the officers that carried out the revolution, since this was up to the military ministries.
86	Cunha, *O Ultramar, a Nação e o 25 de Abril,* p. 357.
87	Lemos, *Duas crises,* pp. 94–95.
88	Carvalho, *O dia inicial. 25 de Abril.,* p. 390. In an interview with Joana Pontes in *A Hora da Liberdade. O 25 de Abril, pelos Protagonistas,* p. 359, Romeiras Júnior mentions that it was he who telephoned Viana Lemos and that he left the house with great care, managing to lose the five officers from the Military Academy who were waiting for him in three vehicles.
89	Carvalho, *O dia inicial. 25 de Abril.,* pp. 391–393.

90 Almeida e Cabral, *25 de abril, memórias*, pp. 64–65. See also interview with Costa Martins in the newspaper *Terra Ruiva* on 11 April 2016, about his own movements on 25 April. http://www.terraruiva.pt/2016/04/11/entrevista-ao-coronel-costa-martins-o-25-de-abril-para-mim-e-uma-forma-de-estar-na-vida/
91 In his memoirs, Américo Thomaz writes that he was warned by Silva Pais at 2:30 am., which does not seem very credible, given that at that time, neither the ministers nor the PIDE/DGS knew of the outbreak of the revolt. Cf. Thomaz, p. 374.
92 Caetano, *O 25 de Abril e o Ultramar*, pp. 41–42.
93 See Diogo de Albuquerque's interview given to Bruno de Oliveira Santos in *Histórias Secretas da PIDE/DGS* (Lisbon: Nova Arrancada, 2000), p. 159.
94 Carvalho, *O dia inicial. 25 de Abril.*, p. 396.
95 In the interview he gave to Adelino Gomes in *Os rapazes dos tanques*, p. 177, Luís David e Silva mentions that he asked Salgueiro Maia if the revolution was under the aegis of General Spínola, to which Maia confirmed that it was, which led the ensign to immediately join the movement.
96 Câmara, *Sanches Osório. Memórias de uma Revolução*, p. 96. Otelo recalls that Salgueiro Maia had reservations about the possibility of arresting the Minister of the Army, given that the latter was a general, while Maia was merely a captain. For this reason, Otelo sent Correia de Campos to Terreiro do Paço to arrest the minister. Interview by Otelo Saraiva de Carvalho with Fátima Campos Ferreira, RTP, 2013. https://www.rtp.pt/play/p9127/e559947/fatima-campos-ferreira-entrevista-otelo-saraiva-de-carvalho
97 Maia, *Aqui Emissora da Liberdade*, p. 89.
98 Carvalho, *O dia inicial. 25 de Abril.*, p. 396.
99 According to David e Silva, the orders to leave came directly from the Under-Secretary of State for the Army, Viana de Lemos. Cf. Cunha, Alfredo, Gomes, Adelino, *Os rapazes dos tanques*, p. 177.
100 Carvalho, *O dia inicial. 25 de Abril.* p. 415; Maia, *Aqui Emissora da Liberdade*, pp. 92–93
101 Cunha, *Ainda o 25 de Abril*, p.126
102 See Caldeira dos Santos' statement given to Maria Flor Pedroso, April 21, 2014. https://www.rtp.pt/play/p1511/e151419/25-herois-do-25 See also report of the events reproduced in the book coordinated by Pedro Lauret, *O Dia da Liberdade. 25 de Abril de 1974*, pp.134–139 and pp. 244–249.
103 In an interview with Joana Pontes, Hugo dos Santos, one of the people responsible for the MFA programme, mentions that some F-86 fighters that were in Monte Real were ready to leave on the MFA's orders. See Pontes, Joana Pontes, Castro, Rodrigo de Sousa e, Afonso, Aniceto, *A Hora da Liberdade. O 25 de Abril, pelos protagonistas*, p. 172.
104 See the various interviews with the protagonists conducted by Adelino Gomes in *Os rapazes dos tanques*, Porto: *Porto Editora*, 2014. According to Jorge Galamba, who at the time worked for the newspaper *Expresso* and who followed these movements, Salgueiro Maia said that he knew Brigadier Reis well, who 'will wage war until five in the afternoon. At five in the afternoon, he fires two or three shots in the air and goes home for tea.' See João Galamba's statement to Adelino Gomes, *Pública* magazine, April 22, 2007.
105 Maia, *Capitão de Abril*, p. 90.
106 Serrão, *Operações Especiais*, p. 116. In Porto, RCP (Portuguese Radio Club) was left without a signal due to a power cut at the Miramar transmitter caused by a technician who switched off the transformer station and ran away with the key. Cf. Maia, *Aqui Emissora da Liberdade*, p. 56.
107 At this moment, the forces that were in Terreiro do Paço were divided into two groups: Salgueiro de Maia's group went to Carmo and another commanded by Jaime Neves went to the Portuguese Legion barracks to obtain their surrender.
108 Carvalho, *O Dia Inicial*, p. 127.
109 Interview given by Salgueiro Maia to Adelino Gomes published in the supplement of no. 664 of the magazine *Fatos e Fotos*, May 1974.
110 Carvalho, *O Dia Inicial*, p. 135.
111 The main opposition force that was in the vicinity of Carmo was the 2nd Squadron of the GNR Cavalry Regiment (about 70 men) commanded by Captain Andrade e Sousa, which was unable to advance because the access roads were cut off and the streets were full of people. Even before the arrival of the forces from Estremoz, this squadron abandoned the fight. Cf. Andrade, *Para Além do Portão. A GNR e o Carmo na Revolução de Abril*, p. 122. See interview given by Andrade e Sousa to Joana Pontes in *A Hora da Liberdade. O 25 de Abril, pelos Protagonistas*, pp. 430–439.
112 Serrão, Joaquim Veríssimo, *Marcello Caetano – Confidências no Exílio*, p. 246.
113 Cunha, *Ainda o 25 de Abril*, p. 127.
114 Cunha, *Ainda o 25 de Abril*, p. 127. According to Viana de Lemos, Andrade e Silva followed in his car, while Silva Cunha and Viana de Lemos went by helicopter. Lemos, *Duas Crises*, p. 97.
115 Interview given by Fernando Velasco to Joana Pontes in *A Hora da Liberdade*, pp. 411–412.
116 AAVV, *25 de Abril, Os 240 que prenderam Caetano, A coluna militar da EPC*, p. 85.
117 Contact had been established between the Secretary of State for Information and Tourism, Pedro Pinto, and Rui Patrício, who was inside the barrack. After this contact, Pedro Pinto then sent Feytor Pinto and Nuno Távora to Carmo. Cf. Pontes, *A Hora da Liberdade*. In his memoirs, Spínola tells that around 02:00 pm, he received Nuno Távora at his house with a message from Pedro Pinto, in which the latter placed himself at his disposal to get in touch with Marcello Caetano. The general refused to intervene arguing that he did not belong to the movement. Later, at 4:30 pm, he received Feytor Pinto and Nuno Távora with Marcello's message, which was confirmed by telephone. Cf. Spínola, *País sem rumo*, pp. 114–115. The moves towards Marcello's surrender were also reported in an article in the *Expresso* newspaper of 27 April 1974. See also Lemos, Mário Matos e, *O 25 de Abril – Uma síntese, uma perspectiva*, pp. 118–121.
118 Interview given by Feytor Pinto to Joana Pontes in *A Hora da Liberdade*, p. 419.
119 MPR/AAS/CX000/0250: Message from Pedro Pinto to António de Spínola commenting on the uprising of 25 April 1974.
120 Pereira, António Maria, *A Burla do 28 de Setembro*, p. 46.
121 Pereira, p. 48.
122 *Expresso* newspaper, 27 April 1974.
123 Personal archive of Luís Campos e Cunha.
124 António de Spínola in *País sem rumo*, pp. 115–116, claims that he received a phone call from Pontinha to go to Carmo to receive the surrender of Marcello de Caetano, however, Otelo in *Alvorada em Abril*, p. 458, argues that it was Spínola who telephoned Pontinha through Lieutenant Colonel Dias de Lima. Spínola remembers having sent Dias de Lima to the Rádio Clube Português to establish contact with the movement's command, and it is possible that Dias de Lima knew how to contact Otelo again.
125 Carvalho, *Alvorada em Abril*, pp. 455–459.
126 The entry into the barracks and the meeting with Marcello Caetano is described in detail in an interview given by Salgueiro Maia to Maria Manuela Cruzeiro in 1991, available on RTP archives. https://arquivos.rtp.pt/conteudos/entrevista-a-salgueiro-maia/
127 Maia, *Capitão de Abril*, p. 96.
128 *Tal & Qual* newspaper, 25 April 1985.
129 Morais, *António de Spínola – O Homem*, p. 78.
130 Testimony of Luís Campos e Cunha, 2022.
131 The vehicle was commanded by furriel Manuel Silva of the Santarém EPC. Marcello Caetano entered through the 'side door' of the vehicle. The furriel admits that he was impressed to see 'in physical presence' the man he had only seen 'in black and white' on television. Manuel Silva recalls that on the way to Pontinha, Caetano kept his 'state posture,' but 'the other two (Patrício and Moreira Baptista) were scared to death.' Testimony of Manuel Silva to Pedro Luís Silva in the newspaper *O Minho*, 25 April 2020. https://ominho.pt/manuel-silva-o-furriel-de-barcelos-que-tirou-marcelo-caetano-do-quartel-do-carmo/
132 The Chaimite V-200, named *Bula*, was the vehicle used to remove the then President of the Council from the Carmo, after the regime's surrender. It was one of two vehicles of this type that formed part of Salgueiro Maia's column. These vehicles were manufactured in Portugal, modelled on the American Cadillac Gage V-100 Commando. The Chaimite V-200 was a light armoured vehicle and amphibious, which was intended to transport troops and had capacity for eight passengers besides the crew of three. Cf. Monteiro, Pedro, *Berliet, Chaimite e UMM – Os Grandes Veículos Militares Nacionais*, pp. 36–37. The three Panhards had the names *Luanda*, *Nova Lisboa* and *Vila Pery*. Cf. Rodrigues, p. 139.
133 Morais, *António de Spínola...*, p. 79.
134 Maia, *Aqui Emissora da Liberdade*..., p. 95 and Serrão, *Operações Especiais*, p. 117. According to the newspaper *República* of 26 April 1974, the clashes in downtown Porto resulted in 17 injuries to civilians and five injuries to the police.
135 Almeida e Cabral, *25 de abril, memórias*, p. 66.
136 Thomaz, p. 375.
137 Silva, Alexandre Pais Ribeiro da, *Capitães de Abril*, p. 153.
138 Crespo, *Porque Perdemos a Guerra*, p. 142.
139 Lemos, *Duas Crises*, pp. 100–101.
140 Morais, *António de Spínola...*, p. 80; Carvalho, *Alvorada em Abril*, p. 471.
141 Carvalho, *Alvorada em Abril*, p. 471.
142 Carvalho, *Alvorada em Abril*, p. 472.
143 Cruzeiro, *Costa Gomes, o último Marechal*, p. 217
144 Charais, Franco, *25 Abril: Golpe Militar ou Revolução?* pp. 33–34.
145 Carvalho, *Alvorada em Abril*, p. 478.
146 The military junta was formed by Commander Rosa Coutinho, Colonel Galvão de Melo, General Costa Gomes, Brigadier Jaime Silvério Marques, Commander Pinheiro de Azevedo and General Manuel Diogo Neto, besides Spínola. All, with the exception of Diogo Neto, who was in service commission in Mozambique, were present in the television broadcast. The broadcast lasted three minutes from 01:26 to 01:29 am in the morning of 26 April, with Spínola reading the MFA proclamation to

147 This military junta was in charge of the country's destiny from Spínola's communiqué, broadcast on public television in the early hours of 26 April 1974, until the first provisional government took office on 16 May of the same year.
148 On 25 April, PIDE shootings caused four deaths and dozens of wounded. A PIDE employee was also killed by a soldier of Cavalry Regiment 3 that night. The death of a PSP agent on 26 April, who was shot by the Marines while travelling in a police van, should also be noted, for a total of six dead. Cf. *A Capital* newspaper of 28 April 1974; Monteiro, Fábio, *Esquecidos em Abril – Os mortos da revolução sem sangue* (Lisbon: Livros Horizonte, 2019).
149 Silva Pais' interview to *Sempre Fixe* on 19 October 1974. In this interview, Silva Pais says that he did not refuse the surrender, given that the previous government had already fallen and that he was thus at the orders of the new power. Sanches Osório confirms that Spínola ordered Moreira Baptista, the former Interior Minister who was imprisoned in Pontinha, to telephone Silva Pais, 'telling him to surrender.' Spínola also spoke to the PIDE director, 'ordering him to cease any resistance, as power was already in the hands of the MFA.' Spínola even told him that, 'if he did not surrender immediately, he would have the PIDE destroyed.' Osório, Sanches, *O Equívoco do 25 de Abril*, p. 43. This version is confirmed by Franco Charais, who was in Pontinha that night. It was Charais who suggested to Spínola to speak with Moreira Baptista to intercede with Silva Pais. Charais, *25 Abril: Golpe Militar ou Revolução?*, p. 33. Otelo also confirms that this was what happened. Cf. Carvalho, op. *cit.*, pp. 472–473.
150 *A Capital* newspaper, 26 April 1974.
151 https://arquivos.rtp.pt/conteudos/conferencia-de-imprensa-da-junta-de-salvacao-nacional/
152 According to an account published in the *Diário Popular* newspaper of 28 April 1974, these contacts began at 07:00 am, when Sergeant Miranda of the Marine force saw an open door in the PIDE/DGS building. He communicated the fact to his superiors and, 'when they came to check what was going on, they found two inspectors of the organisation outside, with whom they immediately made contact, agreeing on the form of surrender.' This version is confirmed by Otelo in *Alvorada em Abril,* p. 482.
153 *Diário Popular* newspaper of 26 April 1974. The *República* newspaper, 26 April 1974, states that the entry into the PIDE/DGS headquarters occurred at 09:45 am and that 'the surrender took place in the presence of elements of the Marine Fusiliers and Infantry Regiment 1, after having sent two PIDE-DGS agents to the interior, previously arrested by the Armed Forces, and that had the mission to convince the entrenched to surrender without conditions.' Costa Correia mentioned that it was only one agent who entered, Costa Azevedo, to guarantee the surrender of the agents who were inside the building. See Testimony of Luís Costa Correia, 2022.
154 There are divergent testimonies about who would have been the first to enter the PIDE/DGS headquarters. Campos Andrada and Alberto Ferreira of the Army argue that their forces were the first to enter the building and only then did the Navy enter. Cf. Alberto Ferreira in *Pronunciamento Militar do 25 de Abril de 1974,* pp. 197–200 and testimonies given to Jacinto Godinho in the documentary *Os Últimos Dias da PIDE*, Episódio 1, RTP, 2014. https://www.rtp.pt/programa/tv/p31738 and to Manuel A. Bernardo in *Equívocos e Realidades – Portugal 1974-1975*, pp. 49–50. Costa Correia, for his part, remembers having seen Campos Andrada join the entourage to enter the PIDE, but admits that Alberto Ferreira could have already been inside. See also in AHM/FO/007/A/34: Memorandum on the Coordination Service for the Extinction of PIDE/DGS and LP, presented to the Council of the Revolution on October 16, 1975, where it is stated that it was a force of Marines that occupied PIDE. The newspapers of the time mention that it was the Navy the first force to enter the headquarters of the political police, although accompanied by Campos de Andrada. Alberto Ferreira would have arrived later. See the report by João Garin in the *Diário de Notícias* newspaper, 27 April 1974. Silva Pais, in an interview written for *Sempre Fixe* on 19 October 1974, also confirms that it was a force of Marines that entered the building.
155 *República* newspaper, 27 April 27 1974; *Diário de Lisboa,* 26 April 1974; statement by Vargas de Matos given to Maria Flor Pedroso, 24 April 2014. https://www.rtp.pt/play/p1511/e151867/25-herois-do-25
156 According to information published at the time in Manuel, Alexandre, Carapinha, Rogério, Neves, Dias (eds.), *PIDE: a história da repressão,* pp. 6–7, the filing cabinets of the political police had about four million files and information about one million Portuguese citizens. As to the number of agents, employees and informers, the number was over 20,000 in total, the high number of informers being noteworthy, given that the organisation itself had only a few hundred agents and employees.
157 *República* newspaper, 27 April 1974. According to this newspaper 228 agents were transferred to Caxias.
158 Rodrigues, *De Súbito em Abril*, p.174. In João Garin's report for the *Diário de Notícias* newspaper of 27 April 1974, the journalist makes no reference to the stepladder.

ABOUT THE AUTHORS

José Augusto Matos is an independent Portuguese researcher focused primarily on air operations during Portugal's colonial wars in Africa. A regular contributor to multiple aviation and naval periodicals, recently wrote a book in Portuguese with Zélia Oliveira about the end of the dictatorship in Portugal in 1974. Matos has also worked on several books in the Helion Africa@War Series and this is his eighth book for Helion.

Zélia Oliveira is a journalist at the Portuguese National News Agency (Lusa) and holds a master's degree in contemporary Portuguese history.